D0948230

£10.95

N&A

The Second Wave

Japan's Global Assault on Financial Services

RICHARD W. WRIGHT

and

GUNTER A. PAULI

Université d'Ottawa
BIBLIOTHÈQUES

LIBRARIES
University of Ottawa

ESIF no. 2

WATERLOW PUBLISHERS

First edition 1987

©Richard W. Wright and Gunter A. Pauli 1987

Waterlow Publishers
Oyez House, PO Box 55
27 Crimscott Street
London SE1 5TS
A division of Hollis Professional and Financial Services PLC

All rights reserved. No part of this publication may be reproduced,
stored in a retrieval system, or transmitted, in any form or by any means,
electronic, mechanical, photocopying, recording or otherwise, without the
prior permission of Waterlow Publishers.

ISBN 0 08 033090 8

HG
3324
.W75
1987

Printed in Great Britain by
A. Wheaton & Co. Ltd, Exeter

To the Osaka Jaycees:

without whom the authors would never have met

Acknowledgements

The task of researching and writing this book would have been vastly more difficult, if not impossible, had it not been for the extraordinarily competent assistance of two individuals: Scott Swallow and Ursula Kobel. The authors express their deepest gratitude. Thanks are due also to Andrew Gates, Joseph Cheung and Lise Grant for their contributions. Finally, an enormous debt of gratitude is owed to the many corporate managers and public officials who gave so willingly of their time to be interviewed in the course of the research. The authors hope that their views and opinions are fairly represented in the final text. A special thanks to Karl Meersman, the young and talented cartoonist who translated many of our ideas into fine cartoons.

Table of Contents

Foreword

by WILLY DE CLERCQ
Member of the Commission of the EC
for External Relations and Trade Policy

Japan is one of the world's leading trading nations and its current structural excess of exports over imports of goods is one of the major headaches for those engaged in international trade policymaking.

Over a period of many years the Japanese have successfully targeted one key sector of manufacturing after another, painstakingly built up an efficient and modern production capability, and proceeded to conquer a major share of world markets. They are respected and feared for their ability to produce reliable products of high quality at an often unbeatable price—in the manufacturing field.

Over the same period this Japanese strength in manufacturing has been traditionally accompanied by a structural weakness in the services field. The massive export surplus on trade in goods has been mitigated by a persistent deficit on the invisibles account.

This important book points out that this situation is now changing. Not only is Japan, as the world's major exporter of capital, now the recipient of an ever-increasing flow of revenues from foreign investment, it is also reducing its relative weakness in services. The genesis of this change, the forces which shape it, and the effects it may have are the subject of this book.

For the European Community, which I have described in the past as the world's "superpower" in services trade (our export receipts from services are more than double those of the United States, four times those of Japan), this is a disquieting message. It threatens to affect the Community strategy of building on the strength of London and other financial centres within the Community through the full realization of a single market of continental dimensions, with a view of making the Community the leading force in world financial services.

This book suggests that this strategy may be threatened by a "second wave" as the Japanese target financial services as their next field of conquest. It comes in time for us to study the wave, understand its dimensions and organize our defences. The challenge to all of us is to construct those defences in time. Before the wave strikes.

Brussels
April 6, 1987

Introduction

Ten years ago the Japanese took the world by surprise with a frontal assault on world consumer electronics, automobile, motorcycle and photographic markets. The techniques that they used in that attack seem almost more appropriate in a military context than in an international business setting; they have even been compared, by the more vocal of the many disgruntled western businessmen, to the techniques used by the Japanese in the attack on Pearl Harbor: stealth, surprise, an unprepared adversary, a specific target, and an overwhelming attack force. The attack temporarily crippled and permanently changed the focus of much of America's consumer electronics industry, virtually eliminated American and British motorcycle production, and sent the U.S. auto industry into a slump that nearly drove Chrysler into bankruptcy. From there the Japanese have taken on countless other western strongholds, including steel, computers and computer components, photographic equipment, electronic watches, etc. The battle over manufacturing supremacy continues unabated, with no sign of a speedy solution to western manufacturers' difficulties.

The Japanese are once again on the move, and a Second Wave of Japanese exports is about to flood the markets of the western world. This time they have targeted the financial services sector as their area of conquest, and once again it appears that the West will be taken completely by surprise. And yet, the signs are all unmistakeably there: a massive cash war-chest flush with funds from a trade surplus which dwarfs even OPEC in its heyday, a government committed to expanding Japan's international financial clout while staunchly protecting the domestic market, and a disciplined, educated population devoted to hard work and self-sacrifice to an extent unrivalled in the West. The Japanese are once again showing the world their ability to take foreign ideas and transplant and perfect them in Japan. Not that this is anything new for the Japanese: they did just that over a thousand years ago when they adopted many of the ideas of the Chinese. In much the same way that smiling Japanese managers toured American automobile plants in the 1950s and 60s, Japanese students visited China in the fifth century A.D.:

> The Japanese leaders, showing extraordinary wisdom for a people only just
> emerging into the light of civilization, carefully chose promising young

1

men to accompany the embassies so that they could study at the sources of knowledge in China. The result was, in a sense, the first organized program of foreign study in the world.(1)

Later, in the late 1800s:

> The Japanese determined to learn from each Western country that in which it particularly excelled. For example, they went to England to study the navy and merchant marine, to Germany for the army and for medicine, to France for local government and law, and to the United States for business methods. The world was one vast schoolroom for them, but they chose what and where they would learn and how they would use the knowledge to change life in Japan.(2)

Sound familiar? Today, through the use of joint ventures or outright purchases of foreign firms, and an intense devotion to studying and mastering the most modern techniques and skills, the Japanese are positioning themselves to become *the* dominant force in international financial services. Already, Japanese banks and securities houses dominate the ranks of the largest of their international peers, with the trend likely to continue in the future, while becoming increasingly adept at mastering the intricacies of the latest financial product innovations. If anything, the conquest of financial services may be even easier than that of automobiles or electronics, because of the worldwide trend towards financial market liberalization and the lack of extensive technological research and capital expenditure required to play the financial services game. If the prospect of a Toyota in every garage frightened you, what about a Nomura Securities office in every city and a Dai-Ichi Kangyo Bank on every corner?

This book draws together for the first time in one place a comprehensive and revealing overview of the challenges posed to the West by Japan's Second Wave. The first three chapters present, in layman's language, important background information for the reader who may not already be familiar with the dynamics of international financial services or with the unique characteristics of Japanese finance. Chapter 4 views Japan's awesome capital surplus position: How has it all come about? What does it mean? The next two chapters focus respectively on Japanese banks and securities companies, identifying their competitive advantages and explaining how they have achieved their positions of dominance. Astutely engineered deregulation of their financial markets (Chapter 7) is one tool by which the Japanese successfully derive maximum gain for themselves. Other means are exposed in Chapter 8: a comprehensive analysis of the competitive strategy of Japan's financial services industry. If the reader requires more evidence of the Second Wave, this chapter provides it, drawing astonishing parallels between the strategy underway to achieve dominance in financial services, and the one used so successfully by the Japanese in information technology.

But the forecasts of doom and gloom need not be realized. The book concludes with practical recommendations to western governments and business firms for meeting the challenge of the Second Wave. The threat is real, and the implications are ominous. How we respond will affect the lives of us all.

1. Edwin O. Reischauer, *Japan: The Story of a Nation*, p. 20.
2. Ibid., p. 135.

CHAPTER 1

Services: Dynamic Force in the World Economy

Services have, until very recently, been largely neglected as a major force in the world economy. The industrialized West has focused mainly on reconverting smokestack industries, launching new high-tech companies, and competing with Japanese and other foreign producers of manufactured goods such as cars and electronics, rather than on the large but less visible services sector. It was not until 1982 that services first received widespread coverage in the international press: the United States government had requested the inclusion of services in the next negotiating round of the General Agreement on Tariffs and Trade (GATT). It came as a surprise to almost everyone. The nebulous area of services remains largely a mystery. What are services? How large are they? How are they changing? How important are they to the economies of industrialized countries, and more to the point, how important are they likely to become?

There still is not even a clear definition of what services comprise. *The Economist* defines services as everything you can buy and sell but not drop on your foot! And the statistics available on the subject are woefully inadequate. While it is easy to identify precisely the different types of potatoes Europe produces, there is not even a subdivision in service statistics for software. When the member governments of the Organization for Economic Cooperation and Development (OECD) agreed to study their services sectors, it took more than two years just to compile a document of only 30 pages on service trade and its barriers. Some countries were months late in supplying their data, putting forward excuses that they did not have the figures on hand, or that their business federations could not formulate clear strategies and positions on the issues.

It has, nevertheless, become increasingly clear that services are *the* engine of growth in the world economy. This is obvious, first, in the number of new jobs created in services over the last decade: nearly 10 million in the United States and some 15 million in the twelve member countries of the European Community.(1) (See Graph 1-1.) As employment is the top priority of every politician, it is amazing that this sector has received so little attention. After all, the industrialized countries of the West will have to develop some 90 million new jobs by the turn of the century just to maintain unemployment at or below 6%.(2)

A second reason for focusing attention on services is the fact that they are the major force for future growth in world trade. At present approximately 24% of world trade is in services. But only 8% of the total

4

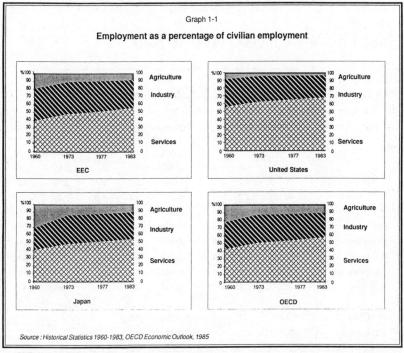

Graph 1-1

Employment as a percentage of civilian employment

EEC — United States — Japan — OECD

Source: *Historical Statistics 1960-1983, OECD Economic Outlook, 1985*

production of services is traded today, in contrast to 45% of manufactured goods and 65% of agroproduce. Thus there is enormous potential for expansion of international trade in services. If, by the end of the present century, services come to be traded at a level comparable to that of manufactured goods today, it will imply double-digit growth over the next two decades. Major countries in world service trade, and recent growth rates, are shown in Tables 1-2 and 1-3.

Although we are all aware of the impact that trade in goods has had on the world economy, the potential for services trade seems clearly underestimated. It was only at the meeting of GATT ministers in Punta del Este, Uruguay in September, 1986 that the member governments finally agreed to put services on the agenda for further negotiations so that one day a set of rules and regulations will apply to trade in services, just as they now do to goods.

There is at least one more important reason to pay attention to services: the Japanese seem to be devoting their highest priority to this sector. Apparently the Japanese believe that they can achieve a sweeping reconversion of their economy by concentrating on services as a major growth sector, in which they possess a set of potential comparative

5

Table 1-2

Major Countries in World Invisible Trade

	Gross invisible receipts (a)						Net Invisible balances	
	1982 US$m	%of world total	Rank	1983 US$m	%of world total	Rank	1982 US$m	1983 US$m
United States	119,364	20.6	1	111,646	21.2	1	48,796	39,810
France	59,905	10.4	2	53,823	10.2	2	7,132	7,379
United Kingdom	45,478	7.9	3	44,497	8.5	3	9,254	9,400
West Germany	*40,197*	*7.0*	*4*	*36,207*	*6.9*	*4*	*-16,306*	*-14,731*
Belgium/Luxemburg	34,768	6.0	5	29,617	5.6	6	1,828	2,986
Japan	*33,032*	*5.7*	*6*	*30,851*	*5.9*	*5*	*-16,880*	*-14,293*
Netherlands	26,810	4.6	7	22,221	4.2	8	184	14
Italy *(b)*	26,168	4.5	8	25,238	4.8	7	2,029	2,938
Switzerland	17,917	3.1	9	17,342	3.3	9	5,974	6,494
Austria *(b)*	12,576	2.2	10	11,957	2.3	10	3,867	3,471
Total 'Top 10'	416,215	72		383,399	72,9			
World Total	578,158	100		526,474	100			

West-Germany and Japan are deficit countries
(a) Excluding miscellaneous government transactions and transfers.
(b) Including miscellaneous government transactions, since not separately identified.

Source: British Invisible Exports Council, 1985

advantages they can use to build up a position of strength similar to that which they have achieved over the last decade in industries such as cars, cameras, electronics and semiconductors. The implications for the West are ominous: history has shown that every time the Japanese have launched such a concerted effort in the past, we North Americans and Europeans have languished in our own sense of invincibility, only to find ourselves poorly prepared to counter their advances into our markets and largely incapable of attacking their home market.

Rise of the Service Economy

Although services have so far not figured prominently in international trade, the countries of the industrialized world have developed highly effective entrepreneurial capabilities in the area of services. The names of

Table 1-3

Growth Index of Total Invisibles 1982 and 1983
(1969=100)

	Receipts		Payments	
	1982	1983	1982	1983
United Kingdom	468	458	511	496
United States	652	610	591	601
Belgium/Luxemburg	1,455	1,239	1,557	1,259
France	1,088	978	1,142	1,005
Italy	516	497	645	596
Netherlands	855	709	1,034	862
West Germany	799	720	739	666
Austria	1,072	1,019	1,118	1,089
Switzerland	818	792	1,291	1,173
Japan	1,280	1,195	1,083	979
World Total	770	701	833	747

Source: British Invisible Exports Council, 1985

some of the leading service companies have even become part of our everyday vocabulary: "Send it DHL," or "Take out a Europ-Assistance insurance policy for your trip," have become catch phrases as common in Europe as "to xerox a document" is in North America.

Table 1-4 lists some of the leading service companies of Europe, the United States, and Japan. It is interesting to note that each region has developed somewhat its own areas of specialization. The leading service companies of Europe, for example, dominate in market segments where we do not (yet) notice much Japanese competition, while Japan leads in areas where Europeans may have large companies, but in which they generally do not claim world market leadership. Some strengths in services arise naturally from the peculiarities of a local environment. It should come as no surprise, for example, that linguistic services rank high on the list of major European service business, constituting a distinct comparative advantage for countries like Sweden, Switzerland and Belgium—after all, where else in the world can you find countries in which a majority of the

7

population speaks at least three languages fluently? Some areas of European strength have arisen late in the services life-cycle, as established companies develop new profit centers to supplement their more traditional activities: Reuters, for example, developed a world position in financial information services where twenty years ago it was considered just a news agency. Other European service companies have emerged as multimillion-dollar businesses from a standing start, thanks to their drive and entrepreneurship. S.W.I.F.T., the communication specialist which now sets the standards for interbank communications, has become a $260 million business after only ten years of operations, and forecasts several more years of double-digit growth as the market continues to mushroom at an explosive rate.

Looking at the list of American service firms, we are probably not surprised that the league of the world's eight largest auditing firms is

TABLE 1-4

Some of the world's leading service companies

Europe's Leading Service Companies		
Berlitz	Switzerland	linguistic services
EF	Sweden	idem
Club Med	France	tourism
Kuoni	Switzerland	idem
Cap Gemini Sogeti	France	software
Logica	UK	idem
Econocom	France	computer related services
Norsk Veritas	Norway	quality and quantity inspection
SGS	Switzerland	idem
East Asiatic	Denmark	trading
Bunge	Belgium	idem
KMG	Dutch/German	auditing
Münchener Rück	Germany	reinsurance
Europ Assistance	France	travel insurance

Vedior Holding	Holland	temporary labor services
Egon Zehnder	Switzerland	executive search
Carré, Orban & Partners	Belgium	idem
Time Manager	Denmark	training
Reuters	UK	information services
Bavarian Studios	Germany	cultural industries
S.W.I.F.T.	Belgium	interbank telecommunications
Saatchi & Saatchi	UK	marketing and advertising

Japan's Leading Service Companies

Asahi Yomiuri Mainichi	media
Dai-Ichi Kangyo Sumitomo Fuji Mitsubishi Sanwa	banking
Nomura Daiwa Yamaichi Nikko	securities house
Nippon Life	insurance
Japan Postal Bank	post office
Japan Travel Bureau	tourism
NYK	shipping
Dentsu	advertising
Nomura Research	research institute
Mitsui Real Estate	property development
JCB	credit cards

America's Leading Service Companies

| American Express
Visa
Diners Club | credit cards |

9

Arthur Andersen Peat Marwick Mitchell Price Waterhouse Arthur Young	audit
Arthur D. Little Booz, Allan and Hamilton McKinsey	consulting
MCI ATT	telecommunications
DHL Emery Federal Express	courier services
AP-Dow Jones Dunn & Bradstreet Gemco (McGraw-Hill) Biosys	financial data bank financial statements data bank transaction data bank medical data bank
American Management Association EDS Nielsen Telerate Disneyland American Hospital Supplies ARA Services American International Underwriters Babcock Citicorp Drexel Burnham Texas Air	executive training systems integrator market research financial information entertainment health care catering insurance engineering banking financial engineers airlines

Source: ESIF, 1986

dominated by Americans, or that the three largest credit card companies are based in the United States. Databank services seem also largely an American domain: 85% of the world's databanks are located in the U.S., with 95% of the profits in this buoyant market generated by just 5% of the companies. As recently as five years ago that market was not even identifiable as a separate business; today it is worth $5 billion a year and is expected to grow at some 35-45% per annum.(3)

But the real shocker comes when we turn our attention away from the West toward the Land of the Rising Sun, where some surprising facts await us: the largest commercial bank in the world is Dai-Ichi Kangyo, and the world's largest securities house is Nomura. And how many of us are aware that the world's largest transportation company (NYK), the largest life-insurance company (Nippon Life), the largest tourism organisation (Japan Travel Bureau), the second-largest advertising agency (Dentsu)... are all Japanese? What's going on here? It is clear that the Japanese have made and are continuing to make a concerted effort to bolster their position in service industries, *particularly those related to finance,* and that they are becoming remarkably successful at beating American and European firms at their own game. How do they do it? Through a competitive strategy based on factors which differ substantially from those of traditional manufacturing industries.

The Basis of Competition

Traditional economic theory prescribes that the comparative advantage of a country, or the competitive edge of a company, depends on the efficient combination of three input factors: capital, labour and raw materials. But when we apply this to services we realize very quickly that services do not have any tangible raw materials as an input. As for capital, studies indicate that the cost of creating a new job in services is only one-tenth to one-twentieth of that in manufacturing industries.(4) And even though the capital investment requirement of some services like banking and retailing is increasing, it remains only a fraction of that needed for assembly plants or semiconductor laboratories. Thus, it seems that the only real input factor is human capital. Indeed, man plays the central role in the competitive edge in any service company—but of course it would be too simplistic to imagine that his input is the only factor.

Two other factors—*organizational technologies* and the *services infrastructure*—also shape the competitive edge of service industries. The importance of organizational technologies may be illustrated by analysing the competitive edge of one of the world's best-known service companies, McDonalds. Preparing a hamburger does not seem to be a very high-tech business. Yet, there is only one company in the world which is able to prepare and sell some four billion hamburgers per year. Human capital is of course important to their success. But so is their unique integration of well-conceived advertising schemes, design and colour combinations, purchasing procedures, quality control, restaurant layouts, product standardization, franchising strategies, etc. Despite all of the competitors emerging on the market, all of the copy-cats that try harder, McDonald's remains the undisputed number one, because nobody else has been able to mastermind a superior mix of organizational technologies.

TABLE 1-5

Examples of organizational technologies

1.	management skills	2.	marketing techniques
3.	distribution networks	4.	training methods
5.	research methodologies	6.	advertising schemes
7.	purchasing procedures	8.	information systems
9.	office structures	10.	design and image
11.	quality assurance	12.	personnel motivation
13.	decision making	14.	after sales services
15.	political engineering	16.	financial controls
17.	contacts and introductions	18.	community programs
19.	media relations	20.	services standardization

This list is not exhaustive and only lists some examples. It is the combination of several points which makes up the organizational technology of a company.
Source: ESIF, 1985

Table 1–5 presents an overview of some organizational technologies, which, depending on the sector, are more or less important in developing a competitive strategy. It is interesting to reflect on the degree to which many of these management techniques have been finely honed in Japanese companies—and the extent to which they have been studied by others as individual functions, but seldom as an integrated system of organizational technologies.

The second input factor which contributes to the competitive edge in service industries is the services infrastructure. Just as manufacturing industries cannot function without an infrastructure of electricty, railways, harbours, sewage systems, water treatment plants, etc. (see Table 1–6), services cannot operate without telecommunications, computer systems, data banks, air transportation, local area networks, value-added networks, ISDN (Integrated Services Digitalized Network, through which voice, data and visual images are transmitted on a single channel), mobile telephones, electronic fund transfers and point-of-sale systems, optic fibers, intelligent buildings (capable of monitoring climate, security, personnel movements, etc), teleports, data highways and service zones. The farmer from Argentina or Australia has for years been able to see his produce being traded on the London Commodity Exchange or the Chicago Mercantile Exchange, thanks to an infrastructure of low-cost transportation and intermediate storage facilities. The provider of services can now look forward also to an infrastructure which will make his service increasingly tradable in a flexible, cost-effective way.

TABLE 1-6

Elements of the industrial and service infrastructure

Industry	Services
1. railways	data highways
2. power stations	computers
3. sewage systems	encryption and security
4. canals	optical fibres
5. harbours	teleports
6. industrial zones	service zones
7. assembly plants	intelligent buildings
8. water treatment plants	telecommunications
9. silos	data banks
10. motorways	VAN's, LAN's and ISDN

Source: ESIF, 1985

In order for services to be tradable, they must first become "transportable" and "storable." Traditional thinking still maintains that services are produced and consumed in the same place and at the same time. A separation of place (transportability) and of time (storability) may still seem utopian, but in fact it is being achieved in many service sectors. Take the library as an example: it offers a service which is traditionally neither transportable nor storable. You have to go to the library, and you are bound by its opening hours. But today we consult data banks: instead of our going to the library, "the library comes to us." The service becomes independent of time and office hours, accessible day or night from any place in the world by anyone possessing a computer, a modem and a telephone line. The transportability and storability of services implies that,

13

for the first time, a service company can expect competition from companies which were not previously able to reach its protected home market, simply because it was not accessible. On the other hand, a dynamic service firm can for the first time now consider the world as its market. This means, in the long run, that consumers will have a much wider choice of service suppliers. Competition will rise, and the quality, variety and flexibility of services will increase dramatically.

In summary, we see in services the rise of a major new thrust of economic activity unforeseen by traditional economists such as Ricardo and Keynes, driven by a set of input factors substantially different from those of traditional, product-based industries. Success in the services sector depends not only on the important human capital, but also on such key factors as organizational technologies and the services infrastructure. The Japanese have studied carefully how they could reverse the only real drain on their economy—the negative trade balance in services—and transform it into a strength. They already possess extraordinary organizational technologies, and they are quickly achieving a highly-developed services infrastructure of computers and communications.

Moving to the Forefront

The market for services is undergoing radical transformations. In western economies otherwise largely stagnant, the outlook in many service sectors is for sustained growth at double-digit rates, with leading service firms doubling their sales, profits, and employment every three to four years.

A first major change is the erosion of the boundaries among traditional services. Banks are engaging in barter trade, writing insurance policies, advising on travel, and engaging in a variety of other new activities. Are the banks in financial services, trading, insurance or tourism? The same applies to other service sectors as well. Marks and Spencer, a British retailer, offers credit cards to its customers—a financial service. Club Med, that epitome of tourism, gives computer courses—that is, training and education. Post offices in Holland sell theatre tickets. These and countless other examples show clearly that the market is increasingly demanding a "one stop service point." This, in turn, allows the service companies to supply more services to their customers, increasing their efficiency and broadening their forms of competition.

A second change is the increased level of standardization of services, again opening new opportunities to firms with vision and foresight. The process of growth in manufacturing depended heavily on the standardization of parts and production processes to achieve high volumes of production and high levels of productivity—a key factor particularly in Japan's manufacturing successes. Similar efficiencies are beginning to be realized in services. This standardization both depends upon and makes possible the integration of new technologies into the services infrastructure. Firms which spot new niches for standardization can create new services. The spectacular success of S.W.I.F.T., for example, is based on standardization of interbank communications.

Still another change is the increasing substitution of services for products, and vice versa—perhaps the most important area for new market-development opportunities. What do we mean by substitution of services and goods? Again, the concept is most easily clarified by examples. The movie theatre provides a service which is consumed at the same time and place as it is offered. It is not a very market-oriented business; after all, the owner decides when, where, and what movie to show. It is not surprising, therefore, that the consumer is opting for an alternative: the video. This product allows him to decide which movie he wants to see, when, and where. In this case, a locally-supplied service is replaced by an internationally-traded good. Thus the Japanese video makers are not just competing against American and European manufacturers, they are actually launching an assault on the movie theatre business as well.

Going the other way, we can illustrate the substitution of a service for a traditional product with the example of books. Fewer and fewer of us consult books when we look for facts and figures. Instead, we consult databanks. Thus the book, a locally-sold good, is replaced by an internationally-traded service, the databank. The databank market has exploded from almost nowhere into a $5 billion business in only a few years, and its growth is almost certain to continue at double-digit rates for years to come. The use of the data banks in France's Minitel system is expanding at the phenomenal rate of 3% per day, with some 2,000 databanks being hooked to the system in less than two years.

Services and industry cannot, of course, be separated; they are interdependent and closely related. But it is clear that services are responsible for the lion's share of value-added in modern economies, moving increasingly to the forefront of industry itself. While automobile manufacturing is still considered mainly a product industry, already 55% of the value added comes from services to the production process. A recent study of the Swiss pharmaceutical industry concluded that by 1990 as much as 82% of the value added in that sector will be created by services.(5)

These many changes illustrate the enormous flux in the present-day market for services. Full of opportunities and challenges, affecting both the service sectors and industry at large, this buoyant economic sector will increasingly define both the comparative advantages of countries and the competitive edges of companies. Services, more than any other economic component, will determine the long-term prospects for trade and employment in the industrialized world. It is imperative that our political leaders recognize their importance and not lag behind the entrepreneurial spirit that is driving the market.

Financial services have until recently been considered the privileged domain of American and European financial houses. The 1.7 million bank employees in Europe, and comparable numbers in North America, constitute one of the largest pools of employment in services. Interest, dividend and capital flows impact heavily on the balance of services trade. It is, consequently, of critical importance that we analyse and prepare ourselves to deal with the challenge that Japanese financial service companies are hurling our way. Quite a few western bankers and securities dealers remain complacent, calling Japan "a first-world industrial state with a third-world financial system." While the Japanese may not yet have the world's most sophisticated financial system, they clearly know how to define and to aggressively pursue competitive niches in a financial services market that is undergoing radical changes.

The following chapter will look more closely at this worldwide revolution in financial services, to help us identify more clearly where and how the Japanese will pursue their assault on the market.

1. European Service Industries Forum, *Report on Services,* (Brussels: ESIF, January 1986).
2. *Employment in the Year 2000* (Mexico City: El Colegio de Mexico, 1982).
3. European Service Industries Forum, *Report on Computer-Related Services* (Brussels, ESIF, October 1986).
4. ESIF, *Report on Services,* op. cit.
5. Ibid.

CHAPTER 2

Financial Services: The Cutting Edge

Of all the service industries, no other is changing at such an astonishing pace as financial services. Sweeping transformations in the regulatory and competitive environments are shaking the very foundations of international finance, generating exciting new opportunities and posing major new challenges for the world's financial institutions. It is into this dynamic arena that the Japanese have launched their Second Wave of international competition, aimed at achieving worldwide pre-eminence in financial services, just as they succeeded earlier in dominating many manufacturing sectors. To understand and appreciate the Japanese challenge, we need to view it in the context of the powerful forces of change reshaping the world of financial services.

Safe and Sound

In his State of the Union address on December 4, 1928 President Coolidge proudly proclaimed:

> No Congress of the United States ever assembled, on surveying the state of the Union, has met with a more pleasing prospect than that which appears at the present time. In the domestic field there is tranquility and contentment...and the highest record of years of prosperity. In the foreign field there is peace, tranquility, the good will which comes from mutual understanding."(1)

In hindsight, the President's words revealed the misguided but pervasive optimism the American people felt regarding the health of their economy. This optimism, coupled with easy access to funds, enticed millions to invest their fortunes in the stock market. Buying on margin became widespread, as many came to believe that stocks could do nothing but appreciate. It was a speculator's paradise.

The great market crash which began in 1929 came as a rude awakening. Its final impact on the economies of America and Europe is hard to estimate. What is certain is that between 1929 and 1932 there were more than 9,000 bank failures in the U.S. alone, with a resulting loss of deposits which amounted to over $7 billion.(2) In the same period unemployment skyrocketed and peaked at around 25%. The traditional mechanisms for controlling the money supply, and through it the economy, such as open-market operations (selling and buying bonds by the government) and adjustment of the rediscount rate, were found to be ineffective.

The crash called for drastic action on the part of the government. Regulation was perceived as a necessary evil to safeguard the interests of the consumer and to minimize the possibility of a similar disaster in the future. In effect, government regulations became the indispensable framework for building the new financial house, resting on the four pillars of commercial banking, securities, trust operations and insurance. Each pillar was to stand on its own; if one pillar collapsed the house would be severely damaged, but would hopefully still stand.

The Glass-Steagall Act, also known as the Banking Act of 1933, was the legal expression of the reform of the American banking industry. Under its terms, the Federal Deposit Insurance Corporation (FDIC) was established, and banks were forbidden to pay interest on demand deposits, to underwrite municipal revenue bonds, or to invest in common stock for their own portfolios. The Securities Act, passed in the same wave of legislation, gave the Federal Trade Commission power to give direction to investment banks concerning appropriate methods of offering and promoting securities. The Securities Exchange Commission was also established "to put a policeman on the corner of Wall Street and Broad."

The shock-waves from the crash travelled beyond the United States and affected virtually every western industrialized country. Security for the investor became a matter of universal concern, and regulation became widely accepted as the appropriate mechanism for achieving this goal. Every industrialized country developed its own set of regulations for its financial services industry.

The search for economic and financial stability extended into the international sphere and eventually resulted in the establishment, after World War II, of an impressive number of agreements and institutions. The Bretton Woods treaty of 1944, for example, substantially reduced exchange rate risks by fixing exchange rates between major trading countries. The reduction of exchange risk was seen as indispensable to the achievement of the two primary post-war economic objectives: full employment and the development of international trade.

Governments' concern with security did have its costs; costs that were, for the most part, absorbed by the consumer. First, regulations impeded the efficient allocation of financial resources by restricting the free flow of funds. Generally, the profit of the financial institutions was dictated by the constraints of regulation and not as a result of catering to market needs in a more efficient way. Second, it was forbidden to establish a multi-purpose financial institution, precluding consequent savings through reduced overhead. Each of the four permitted types of institution inevitably passed the cost of its own overhead to the consumer. Third, regulation reduced investment flexibility for the consumer of financial services. It removed the incentive for financial institutions to develop a wide range of products because each type of institution had, in effect, a captive market. Correspondingly, the consumer's choice of financial instruments was limited. Lastly, someone had to develop and enforce the regulations. By the 1950s there were more than 60 agencies and 100,000 people directly involved in the regulation of industry in the United States alone.

Within the framework of regulation, financial institutions prospered and became stable pillars of the economy. Regulation encouraged the maintenance of a conservative outlook. Recently, the Governor of the Bank of England, speaking at a colloquium in London, reminded the participants that "it was not such a very long time ago when the advice given to bankers was 'never be first'". Meeting the consumer's needs through innovation was not considered by the financial institutions as particularly necessary.

A Rolling Stone . . .

No system, no profession, can remain stagnant indefinitely. Sooner or later, external forces acting on the system will break down the traditional walls and force change. In the financial services industry the panoply of national rules and regulations on savings, investment, foreign exchange, interest, and a variety of instruments did not always serve the needs of governments and companies which had to follow shifts in the world markets. The limitations of "safe n'sound" policies became apparent and changes started taking place in the early 1950s.

The British government was one of the first to identify and cater to the desire of consumers (in this case large institutions and governments) for more efficient and flexible financial instruments. The Bank of England, however, was not willing to jeopardize the stability of the pound sterling by subjecting it to the forces of supply and demand. It arrived at what was thought to be a clever compromise: adopting a *laisser-faire, laisser-passer* attitude on specific large financial transactions, providing that the transactions were not expressed in pounds.

By the end of the 1950s the Eurodollar was created and the development of modern-day international banking began in earnest. The Eurodollar was a product innovation created by a well-run East-block bank, La Banque Commerciale pour l'Europe du Nord (cable code "Eurobank").

The Eurobank had acquired sizable U.S. deposits and needed a way to place dollar-dominated assets without risk of American reprisals. The Eurobank made these funds available to the European banking community. The banks were delighted because they gained access to new and cheaper funds: Eurodollars fell outside nationally-legislated reserve requirements and therefore could be loaned and reloaned almost *ad infinitum*. They became pure financial tools for operations which in eight or nine cases out of ten had no physical transfer of goods as a basis. Governments too were pleased because they had access to these new funds and, in addition, the value of their currency was not directly affected.

Another major impetus to the internationalization of the banking industry came in the 1970s when western banks received massive deposits from the OPEC nations. This new source of funds led the banks to seek out debtors who needed large volumes of financial assistance and from whom the banks could obtain the best spreads at the lowest risk. Much of the OPEC surplus was recycled by way of syndicated loans to less-developed countries (LDCs): LDCs offered the attractive spreads wanted by the banks because their demand for funds was high and the price of their raw materials, from which they could repay the loans, was also high. And because countries in theory can't go bankrupt, risk was perceived as low. Many European and North American banks became truly international institutions, generating more than half of their profits abroad.

Today, the number of foreign banking institutions provides concrete evidence of the extent to which the banking sector is internationalized. In a country as small as Belgium, for example, there are 86 registered banks. Of these, only 17 are Belgian banks with majority-Belgian participation. The others, all foreign banks, subsidiaries of foreign banks, or registered Belgian banks with majority foreign participation, together account for 51% of the total assets of the Belgian banking system, according to the latest report of the Banking Commission. Add to that the fact that even for those Belgian banks with majority Belgian participation, foreign transactions account for fully one-third of total operations. Even in such a small country, not considered one of the world's major financial centres, internationalization is strikingly evident. The statistics are similar elsewhere. There are, at the last count, approximately 293 foreign banks in London; in Paris there are 147; in Germany 287; and in the U.S. the agencies and branches and other affiliates of foreign banking institutions number 783.

Gaining Momentum

The financial rolling stone is gaining momentum. The financial services industry today is fundamentally different from the industry twenty or even ten years ago. The industry faces many new challenges and opportunities. Consumers, large and small, in their quest for high return and flexibility, have began shopping around for their financial goods. Financial institutions are quickly shedding their conservative outlook and are trying to respond to the needs of the consumer. Product innovation has become a prerequisite for the survival of all financial institutions. The creativity of financial specialists has even led to the addition of a new and imaginative vocabulary to the financial lexicon: a junk bond, a vanilla swap, a samurai bond, a strawberry flat deal, etc. Technology has made it possible to transcend international boundaries and to manipulate volumes of information never before possible. Regulations are being removed, slowly in some countries, more rapidly in others. The classical distinction between the different sectors is becoming blurred as the different sectors vie for each others' traditional line of business.

The four pillars are not crumbling, but they are changing. A new house is being shaped by the combined forces of *securitization, deregulation,* and *innovation* in products and technology, as explained below. The rapid changes in the environment are also producing some interesting side effects: mergers and acquisitions, headhunting, and even re-regulation.

Greener Pastures

Banks are no longer the cheap source of capital they once were. The bankers' panacea of the seventies, the LDC loan, has not performed at all in the way bankers expected. LDCs are struggling to deal with internal economic problems as well as lagging export income caused by depressed prices for primary commodities. Loans made to LDCs are being rescheduled or even partially written off.

These bad debts have put many banks in a straight jacket. Bank credit ratings have dropped, making it expensive for banks to obtain new funds. Many clients of the banks have better credit ratings than the banks themselves. These non-banking institutions are finding that they can obtain funds from the capital markets at terms more favourable than their banks can. The dilemma facing the banks is obvious: their costs of capital have risen to the point where their traditional line of business, corporate lending, is no longer cost competitive.

Many large institutional borrowers have decided to bypass the banks (thus *disintermediation* occurs) and are sourcing funds directly from the market by issuing bonds or stock (*securitization*). For the borrower, securitization of debt is not only attractive in terms of cost, it allows the borrower to spread his risk among numerous lenders and, unlike a loan, an equity issue does not appear as a liability on the corporate balance sheet.

Considerable shifts in credit operations have already occurred. Syndicated Eurocurrency loans, which were at one time the prevailing vehicle for large international credits, decreased fourfold between 1981-82 and the first half of 1985, from $100 billion to a mere $25 billion, and, during the same period, the international issuance of bonds and securities quadrupled, from $44 billion dollars to an estimated $160 billion.

Securities companies have become a major benefactor in the trend towards the securitization of debt. Institutional borrowers require the services of the securities firms for underwriting purposes. Securitization has also vastly increased the number and complexity of financial instruments available. The result: investors are increasingly turning to the securities firms for advice on such things as new products, equity valuation, and the impact of currency fluctuations on their portfolios.

In the process the securities companies are becoming as internationalized as the banks. As an example, the number of foreign securities firms with branches in Tokyo increased from three in 1980 to 23 at the end of 1986. There are now more foreign securities firms with representative offices in Tokyo (124) than there are foreign bank representative offices there (123).

Let 'em Loose

Few things can have a greater potential impact on a market-place than changing the rules of the game. Governments the world over are *deregulating,* or removing the rules which traditionally separated the four financial sectors. The financial system of today has become large and complex. In general, governments are adopting the view that regulation has become excessive and is not required to ensure a secure financial system. Furthermore, excessive regulation is leading to inefficiencies that are not in the best interests of the consumer.

In the banking industry, Britain and the Netherlands have been the leaders in deregulation. In both countries, sector-specific regulations such as credit ceilings, interest-rate controls, and branching restrictions have long been removed. Banks in these countries are also relatively free to participate in traditionally non-banking activities such as the underwriting of securities and real estate investments. Britain recently made sweeping changes to its security regulations, abolishing the fixed commission fees charged for securities transactions and, more importantly, giving banks, foreign and domestic alike, the right to purchase securities directly from the market. The day the changes went into effect was called the Big Bang: the flurry of activity was so great that even the new super computers were unable to cope.

In the United States and Japan the banking industry is still burdened with varying degrees of regulation. In the United States, banks were first allowed to act as discount brokers in 1981; by early 1986 purchase of local banks by out-of-state banks was allowed in 26 out of 50 states; and the interest cap on passbook savings was removed in April 1986. American banks have, however, so far been denied such freedoms as the right to manage or underwrite life insurance, or to manage mutual funds. Among the major industrialized powers, Japan has by far the most restricted financial services sector. We discuss regulation in Japan at greater length in chapter 7.

Innovations upon Innovations

In response to the opportunities created by securitization and deregulation, financial institutions, large and small, have taken to developing their own innovative new financial instruments. Products are being developed for the full spectrum of consumers, from the large institutional investor to the man in the street. The common theme with all these new products and services is that they are cheaper and more flexible than their predecessors.

Perhaps one of the most significant services developed for the institutional client in recent years has been the *swap*. A swap, in simple terms, is a trade of debt, interest or principal, between two parties. The transaction, usually arranged by a financial intermediary, is based on the theory of competitive advantage. If party A, for example, has an abundant supply of yen debt but wishes to balance his holdings with some dollar debt, and party B, conversely, has an abundant supply of dollar debt and wishes to acquire some yen debt, then a mutually-beneficial trade can be arranged. A similar type of arrangement can be arranged for clients who have comparative advantages in either floating- or fixed-interest debt. Although the figures on the swap business are sketchy, volume has grown from about $5 billion in 1983 to roughly $200 billion in 1986.(3)

As mentioned earlier some of these new financial products carry some rather colorful names. For clients who wish to make a straight trade of debt there is the vanilla swap. Those wishing something more exotic may go for a strawberry flat deal. A company involved in a large corporate takeover will in all likelihood finance part of the deal by issuing low-grade unsecured debt, hence the term junk bond. These and other creative financial instruments yet to be developed will ensure the highest possible service levels for clients, while providing outstanding returns and growth avenues to the firms willing to take the substantial risks of committing resources to developing them.

The man on the street has also benefited from product innovations. In retail banking, which is feeling the pinch of securitization and deregulation, consumers are receiving better rates of interest on their deposits than ever before. The banks have also begun bundling up such asssets as mortgages, car loans and consumer loans and then selling marketable securities on the strength of the bundle. This product innovation frees up funds for the banks and enables them to issue loans, at better terms, to the consumer. To maintain their customers, the insurance companies are now providing insurance plans whose savings portion is more in tune with current market returns.

Going High-Tech

Many of the new products and services that have been created owe their birth to developments in technology, which have made it possible to eliminate inefficiencies in the market place. In the past some retailers, for example, had great reservations about the loss of interest caused by the banks' slow processing of checks. These retailers pushed for technology that would circumvent this problem by permitting the electronic transfer of funds directly from the point of sale. EFTPOS, the Electronic Funds Transfer from the Point of Sale, is the name that has been given to the technology that was developed. A similar process occurred with automatic teller machines (ATMs). The banks had to respond to the long lineups at tellers' counters during business hours, a situation that was causing both the public and bank personnel considerable frustration. ATMs were an attractive solution. They gave the consumers the flexibility to withdraw funds at different locations, often during non-banking hours. They also allowed banks to reduce their administrative costs by allowing consumers to perform basic banking functions without the assistance of bank personnel.

Technology has also made possible the development of new, sophisticated financial products. In the past, for example, being a bond portfolio manager meant keeping a close watch on the credit worthiness of borrowers and monitoring macro-economic variables. With interest rates now far less stable than they once were (a bond's value is inversely

24

related to moves in the interest rate), and with a vast new array of products created as a result of securitization, the process has become far more complex to manage. Simple maximization of portfolio value is no longer adequate; better results can be had by "dedicating" or matching bond revenues to future liabilities. For example, a portfolio might be established to pay for our retirements. Dedicating the portfolio's returns against when we want our pension checks ensures that money is available when needed, minimizes dealer costs, and maximizes overall profitability. To achieve all of this, companies have taken to hiring people competent with complex quantitative information and computers: Ph.Ds in such disciplines as quantitative methods, pure mathematics, and computer science. The whole process has become largely dependent on the computer's ability to "crunch" millions upon millions of numbers.

Much of the technology adopted by financial institutions has become accepted and is emerging as the basic infrastructure of the industry. For example, a decade ago there were no ATMs; By 1985 there were 60,000 machines in the U.S. alone and two new machines are being added every hour. The volume of business made possible as a result of technology is astonishing. In 1985, during the average business hour in the United States, approximately:

—14 million personal cheques were written;

—7,000 new bank accounts were opened;

—22,000 airline tickets were purchased by consumers using either bank, travel, or entertainment card;

—45,000 insurance policies were written;

—more than 1,000 money-market fund and money-market deposit accounts were opened.(4)

It is not surprising therefore to learn that financial institutions have already invested huge sums in new technology. It is estimated that between 1980 and 1985, the large American banks spent $7 billion upgrading their technology.(5) Investments of similar proportions have been made by retail banks of other industrialized countries. The cost of computerization and networking has become the second biggest expenditure of banks, after personnel.

The same holds true for the securities industry. In Japan, for example, Nomura Securities plans to spend $400–500 million on developing NEWTON: Nomura Electronic World Wide Total Online Network. Nomura will be able to bring the computer into the homes and offices of its clients. In the words of Nomura's president Yoshihisa Tabushi: "The online system will not only include the retail banking system but will also

25

be integrated with the international network capable of 24-hour trading."(6)

The 24-hour market referred to by Mr. Tabushi, or the "global capital market," is technically feasible today. Debt markets are already, to a great extent, global. Eurobonds are actively traded worldwide. The consumer has become familiar with the advantages of international travellers checks. In 1986, for example, Thomas Cook Financial Services sold over 100 million checks through a network of some 150,000 agents around the world.(7) These checks in turn were cashed in over 180 countries. Again technology played a significant role in making this possible.

Originally, financial institutions purchased equipment based on recommendations made by the various producers of the technology. Consequently, they acquired a wide variety of non-compatible systems which perform essentially the same functions. Now it is the buyers and users of the technology who are pushing for the next logical step in the development of technology: the standardization or compatibility of one system with another. With the globalization of the financial markets the pressure is on to standardize technology, not only nationally but internationally.

There has been substantial progress. Prior to 1977, for example, the international settlement of accounts between banks was largely carried out by mail or telex. The process was slow, because each bank had its own procedures. In a cooperative effort between banks, a standardized telecommunications network, called S.W.I.F.T. (Society for Worldwide Interbank Financial Telecommunications) was created. S.W.I.F.T. now handles over 850,000 transactions daily through 2,472 member banks in 65 countries.(8) S.W.I.F.T.'s success has forced other clearing systems such as CHIPS (Clearing House Interbank Payments System) and CHAPS (Clearing House Automated Payments System) to develop interfaces that allow them to link up to S.W.I.F.T.

The future of such propositions as the universal bank card and the global equities market is no longer restricted by limitations in technology. Rather, the speed at which such developments take place will be determined largely by the ability of different organizations to band together and standardize their procedures and their technologies.

Side Effects

The environment in which the financial services industry operates is changing rapidly. Side effects, all of which have their own importance, are bound to occur. As is the case with the morning after, it is sometimes difficult to identify the cause of pain: was it the vodka, rum, and gin, or was it that tumble down the stairs? *Mergers and acquisitions, corporate raiding*, and *re-regulation* are some of the important consequences of the heady brew of deregulation, disintermediation and innovations in products and technology.

"I liked the razor so much that I bought the company." These familiar words of Victor Kiam, President of Remington, are in fact a good indication of what has become common practice in many industries and in many countries around the world: if you don't have the expertise, the product, or the economies of scope and scale needed to compete successfully in today's corporate jungle, the simplest solution is to acquire someone who does. Nowhere is this philosophy more apparent than in financial services. The reasons are simple. Innumerable opportunities exist for financial institutions to profit from the changes that are sweeping the industry. However, capitalizing on these opportunities requires an appropriate blend of personnel, capital, and infrastructure. Many companies do not have this blend, and the quickest way to acquire it is through *merger or acquisition*. The list of institutions which have been involved in mergers and acquisitions is long: prominent examples include Sumitomo Bank, Barclays Bank, Chase Manhattan and Kleinwort Benson.

The melting of corporate cultures can, however, create difficulties. Acquisitioners have taken to placating acquisitionees by offering such pacifiers as new Porsches, signing bonuses (between $100,000 to $500,000 is not uncommon), and healthy pay raises. Many employers are finding this trend a bit hard to take, particularly given the fact that one's investment can get up and walk away. There have been casualties. In March 1986, Kleinwort Benson Ltd. paid $44 million for the stockbroker Grierson Grant & Co. Virtually the next day Grierson's five-man financial team left for Morgan Grenfell & Co. Ltd., Kleinwort Benson's major British merchant bank competitor.

Japanese companies are also acquiring or merging with American and European companies. Domestically they have shown a strong distaste for hostile takeovers. Perhaps nowhere in the world is corporate culture as strong as in Japan, However, the bottom-up rationalization of the securities industry is taking place there also. In 1949, there were 1,127 domestic securities companies operating in Japan. Currently, some 200 remain.(9) Of these, four have emerged as market leaders: Nomura, Daiwa, Nikko, Yamaichi. Many of the smaller securities companies have established relationships with large Japanese banks. Supposing that substantial liberalization of the Japanese financial services industry will occur, many of the smaller securities companies already have bigger brothers to whom they will be able to turn.

Another alternative to the complete merger or acquisition is to selectively hire away personnel from other companies. *Corporate raiding* for people in key positions has become almost a standard practice. Unfortunately, as is the case with mergers, the up-front costs can be high and, if one is not careful, one's investment can be lured away by another, more attractive offer.

So far the Japanese have proved relatively immune to the corporate headhunting game. The loyalty of Japanese to their companies is still of paramount importance. Japanese managers do get substantial pay raises when they are transferred abroad. However, their wage levels often remain 50% below those of their non-Japanese counterparts. Despite this, Japanese firms are actively recruiting non-Japanese talent abroad, and they are paying more than prevailing market rates for it.

Despite all the talk about deregulation, governments around the world have not lost sight of the importance of regulation or *re-regulation*. Many policy makers are in fact quite perturbed at the difficulties in monitoring the rapid developments that are taking place in industry. Financial transactions are becoming so complex and geographically mobile that it has become exceedingly difficult to establish controls where controls are needed. Securitization, and the corresponding off-balance-sheet nature of many new financial instruments, has made it particularly difficult to assess from reported balance sheet data the actual exposure a particular entity has.

Central bankers are among those that have expressed the greatest concern. Steps are being taken to monitor more effectively the rapid changes in the market place. But in the words of Sam Y. Cross, Executive Vice-President of the Federal Reserve Bank of New York: "The issues are complex and the progress is likely to be slow".

While for the regulators the progress has been slow, the financial institutions are proceeding at full bore, developing new products and services to meet the needs of their clients. The sweeping forces described in this chapter are dramatically reshaping the arena of international financial services, and the Japanese are moving aggressively to position themselves at center stage. To respond effectively to their challenge, we need first some understanding of how Japanese finance works. The next chapter describes that topsy-turvey world.

1. John Kenneth Galbraith, *The Great Crash, 1929* (Boston: Houghton Mifflin, 1954), p. 6.
2. Frances E. Wrocklage, "Banking in the Depression," *Banking,* October 1975, p. 150.
3. "A Survey of Corporate Finance," *The Economist,* June 7, 1986, p. 4.
4. "International Banking Survey," *The Economist,* March 22, 1986, p. 15.
5. Ibid.
6. "The Grand Strategy of Nomura," *Asian Finance,* August 15, 1986, p. 55.
7. Sean Heath, "Thomas Cook Financial Services: Smart Moves Ahead," *Banking Technology,* July 1986, p. 28.
8. *SWIFT Monthly Newsletter,* November 1986.
9. "The Small Openings for Security Companies," *Far Eastern Economic Review,* August 7, 1986, p. 54.

CHAPTER 3

Japanese Finance: Topsy Turvy

As the world's financial markets become more internationalized, the capital markets and corporations of Japan assume an increasingly prominent role. To the outsider, financial practices and relationships in Japan appear to reasonably resemble those of many western countries. Indeed, the foundations of the modern-day Japanese financial system were built by General Douglas MacArthur and his American Occupation staff after World War II, for the purpose of redistributing the shares of the old *zaibatsu* holding companies to the Japanese public. The Japanese financial exchanges were based on American models, and the Japanese agreed to generally-accepted accounting principles prevailing in the U.S. On the surface, then, it would seem that westerners should have little difficulty understanding and interpreting Japanese financial institutions and practices within a familiar framework.

But behind this institutional and legal facade which the Americans imposed, traditional Japanese financial relationships remain deeply entrenched. Japanese financial services have characteristics profoundly different from those of North America or Europe. Such key features as the relationship between financial institutions and their corporate clients, the role of debt financing, and the valuation of equities are unique to Japan.

Viewing Japanese financial services through traditional western assumptions can yield wildly misleading interpretations and conclusions. If we try to explain competitive strategies of individual Japanese companies in the context of the near-term profit-maximizing objectives we expect of private businesses in the West, we see behavior that seems bizarre. If we examine the leverage and cash flow ratios of Japanese corporate balance sheets, we conclude that most large Japanese companies are on the brink of bankruptcy. If we look at the price/earnings ratios prevailing on Japanese stock exchanges, it seems that a major bust must be imminent.

Economic Interest Groups

One of the first mistakes made by westerners viewing Japanese business is the assumption that business organizations are independent entities, as they are in most other industrialized countries. In fact, Japanese business is dominated by a dozen or so huge clusters of companies, each linking vast numbers of complementary industrial and financial entities together into networks of cooperative interdependencies almost totally unique to Japan.

The modern-day "families" of companies had their origins in the pre-World War II *zaibatsu* or giant clusters of companies from many different industries. Each conglomerate was formally tied together by a common holding company and interlocking directorships. Under pressure from the American occupation authorities, who viewed such groupings as incompatible with American anti-monopoly ideals, the *zaibatsu* were formally dissolved after the war. But tradition does not change that easily. Almost as soon as the American occupation forces had left Japan, the old groups began moving back together, only this time on a more informal basis: voluntary associations of apparently independent companies from a wide range of different industries.

Striking evidence of the groups' resurgence is the decline in the importance of individual investors, as Japanese business and financial institutions moved back into their tightly-knit clusters with interlocking shareholdings. Individual investors held 40% of all Japanese shares in 1970; by 1984 that proportion had declined to only 26% (see Figure 3-1).

At first, the large Japanese general trading companies replaced the earlier holding companies at the nucleus of each of the groups. The Japanese have always placed heavy emphasis on *security* in their business and financial dealings. The dominant need of Japanese industry in the immediate post-war period was to gain secure sources of raw materials and to build distribution channels abroad. As the organizations best equipped

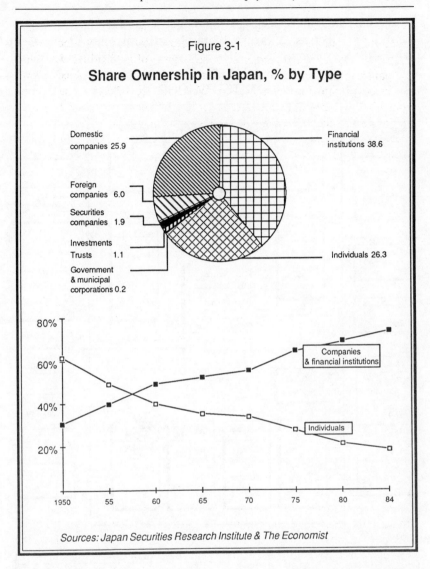

Figure 3-1

Share Ownership in Japan, % by Type

Domestic companies 25.9

Financial institutions 38.6

Foreign companies 6.0

Securities companies 1.9

Investments Trusts 1.1

Government & municipal corporations 0.2

Individuals 26.3

Companies & financial institutions

Individuals

Sources: Japan Securities Research Institute & The Economist

to provide the needed expertise, it was logical that the trading companies would at first assume the key strategic position within each group. Over time, however, as those initial security needs were increasingly satisfied, sustained and reliable financing for expansion became the paramount concern, and the large commercial banks began to assume the key, coordinating role at the core of each group.

33

The influence of these clusters on Japanese industry and finance is powerful and pervasive. Figure 3-2 displays the structure of one such family, the Mitsui group. Now referred to as *keiretsu,* or informal groups,

Figure 3-2

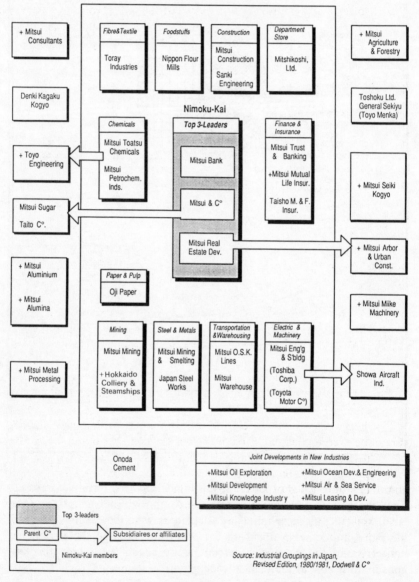

MITSUIGROUP

Source: *Industrial Groupings in Japan,*
Revised Edition, 1980/1981, Dodwell & C°

each of these major clusters resembles a massive spider web, with one of the major Japanese commercial banks at its center. Although each company affiliated with an interest group is ostensibly a separate legal entity, they are bound together in a vast array of informal cooperative relationships.

First off, all of the business firms associated with a group use as their main bank the commercial bank at the core of that group. In addition, small amounts of the shares of each of the member companies are owned by that cluster's bank, by its pension funds, and by the other industrial firms comprising the group. Although the ownership by one member company of shares of any other member company seldom exceeds 5%, when all of the bits and pieces are added together, effective ownership and control of each company is held collectively within the family. There is no longer a central board of directors providing common leadership to the group, but it is customary for the presidents of each of the major affiliated companies to meet informally on a regular basis to coordinate strategy and to discuss problems of common interest. The member companies do a great deal of their business with each other: as much as 50% of the total volume of business done by members of the groups is with other members of the same group. If any individual company associated with a group gets into temporary business or financial adversity, it is expected that other member companies will come to its aid by extending trade credit, by granting loans, and even by providing managerial assistance.

The *keiretsu* provides a huge and enormously diversified base over which to spread the risks of launching new enterprises and moving in new strategic directions—not through legal obligations, but through informal consensus—which is unmatched in any other country. Their existence means also that "sunset" industries which lack international competitiveness can be faded out with minimal trauma, as both physical and human assets can usually be absorbed elsewhere among the members of the "family."

The importance of these clusters of companies to Japanese finance cannot be overemphasized. First of all, western concepts of the separation of industrial firms and financial institutions are largely irrelevant. Although Japanese banks are limited by law to holding only small amounts of the shares of the companies they lend to (unlike in Germany, for example), the interlocking ownership structure of the Japanese business groupings means that any financial transactions with members of the same cluster are really dealings within the "family." The bonds of long-term loyalty and mutual self-interest between industrial firms and financial institutions are probably stronger in Japan than anywhere else.

35

This means that the Japanese banks have a very large and extremely secure client base domestically. It means also that they have the assurance of prior access to the business of their related industrial firms even when the latter expand abroad. Another important consequence of the close traditional relationship between banks and industrial firms is that Japanese banks have inside, proprietary access to managerial and technological developments within their related client companies. Indeed, in most of the groups the commercial banks play a key role in defining and directing the strategic plans of their corporate clients. They also have immediate access to technological developments from a wide variety of industries, including home electronics, telecommunications and computer technology, all of which may be applied directly to the global expansion of the financial services industry itself.

The cooperative relationships binding together the members of a Japanese industrial group are informal and subtle. But their influence is profound. The foreigner failing to appreciate their pervasive role will almost certainly fail to understand the behavior of industrial firms and financial institutions alike. As one knowledgeable foreigner with years of experience in Japan puts it: "You may feel you are dealing on a one-to-one basis with an individual company...but there is no such thing as an individual company in Japan."

The Role of Debt

One of the most striking features of concern to western lenders and investors viewing Japan is the extremely high financial leverage of Japanese companies. By measures of financial soundness traditionally used in western countries, risk exposures almost inconceivable elsewhere prevail in Japanese business finance. Although reliance on debt has edged down slightly in recent years, it is still common for borrowed funds to exceed owners' equity in large Japanese companies by a multiple of five or six times, far higher than in other industrialized countries (see Table 3-3). Similarly high risk complexions are suggested by other financial statement measures such as interest coverage and cash flow coverage.

Are so many Japanese companies teetering on the brink of financial disaster as their financial statements would suggest? Appearances are deceiving. To understand the true nature of financial structure and financial risk in Japan, we have to look well beneath the surface, to the unique financing practices of Japanese companies and to the unique lending practices of Japanese banks.

Table 3-3

Debt-to-equity ratios

Seven arbitrary selected industries in the United States, West Germany and Japan.

Ratios based on book value

Industries	US	West Germany	Japan
Chemicals	0.76	1.37	4.37
Steel	1.82	4.74	6.17
Data Processing	0.67	0.27	1.09
Electrical and Electronics	0.77	5.17	3.01
Machinery and Engineering	1.09	1.88	5.47
Motor	2.03	1.29	1.50
Airlines	1.39	1.61	3.81
Average	*1.22*	*2.33*	*3.63*

Ratios based on market value of equity

Industries	US	West Germany	Japan
Chemicals	0.58	0.70	1.09
Steel	3.32	2.84	4.05
Data Processing	0.45	0.44	0.40
Electrical and Electronics	0.04	2.16	1.53
Machinery and Engineering	0.91	0.87	2.19
Motor	1.73	0.45	1.19
Airlines	1.35	0.52	0.51
Average	*1.25*	*1.14*	*1.57*

Source: Morgan Stanley Capital International & The Economist

Why Companies Have Borrowed So Heavily

A basic feature of Japanese business has been its objective of growth. Particularly during the high-growth period of the 1950s and 1960s, Japanese managers believed that massive investment in expanding size and output would contribute to higher cash inflows in the future. But it was difficult for companies seeking to maintain their market share to accumulate sufficient capital out of earnings, even with full retention of profits. Thus, increasing dependence on external funds was inevitable.

In choosing among the various sources of external funds (borrowing, bonds, stocks), tax deductibility of interest unquestionably favored debt financing. But the strong traditional Japanese bias toward debt is not explained sufficiently by taxes, because roughly comparable tax burdens in other countries have not led to comparable corporate financing decisions.

More important was the unique stock issue system prevalent in Japan during most of the post-war growth period and continuing, to a limited extent, today. Under this system, all stocks were issued at par value (generally 50 yen per share) regardless of market prices. Larger companies were expected to pay a dividend of 10-15% of par value to maintain a respectable corporate image. Thus, corporate financial managers seeking low-dividend-burden funds were constrained by the traditional practice of stock issue at par.

Even for those large firms which began, in the 1970s, to issue stocks at or near market value, the explicit cost of equity funds, as viewed by management, remained high. Under a voluntary rule enforced by the major securities companies, issuing companies were required to return all of the premium between par and issue price to the shareholders in the form of free distribution of shares, over a period of five years. These free shares were distributed not only to new shareholders but also to existing shareholders. By increasing the dividend burden in the future, the practice of free distribution of shares negated most of the additional benefit of market-price issues in the long run. The rule discriminated particularly against highly capitalized companies that already had a large number of outstanding shares.

New rules governing stock issues and dividend payments have added more flexibility to equity issues in Japan, and equity ratios in Japanese industry are rising slowly over time. But the historical need of Japanese companies for major external financing, combined with numerous regulations making frequent use of equity markets difficult and costly, help to explain why most Japanese companies have relied so heavily on the most convenient and abundant source of funds: bank loans.

Of course, conditions change, and the security needs of Japanese industry change with them. Financial relationships which sustained Japan's spectacular economic growth through the mid-1970s are less appropriate to today's slower-growth environment. During the high-growth period, the main security concern of industry was a reliable, sustained supply of external funding to fuel the investment demands of rapid growth. This the commercial banks could provide. But in the present environment of moderate growth and greater economic uncertainty, security is realized more by a strong financial structure which offers a protective buffer in times of adversity, such as the rapid rise of the yen. Accordingly, Japanese industry is turning increasingly from the banks toward the Japanese securities companies to provide them with equity financing instruments and with funding from Western European and North American markets.

Why Banks Have Lent So Much

The desire of Japanese companies to raise vast amounts of funds from borrowed sources has been facilitated by the unique lending practices of the commercial banks. The arms-length, competitive principles of North American and European-style banking do not exist in Japan's clannish, cooperative business society. The *zaibatsu* holding companies that controlled large clusters of firms were broken up at the end of World War II; but the largest banks have, in effect, replaced them in their function as leaders of the *keiretsu* groups, a role that calls for ties and capabilities not normally associated with the concept of commercial banking. Thus, banks in Japan are much more closely involved with their borrowers over the long run than are commercial banks elsewhere. Lending, while ostensibly short term, is rolled over automatically to create long-term financing; banks continue lending in times of financial adversity for a borrower; loans are almost never recalled. The closeness of the lending relationship itself is reinforced by the banks' holding of bonds and common stocks of the companies to which they lend. It is common also for the banks to send officers directly into the top management of corporate borrowers in financial difficulty.

The heavy lending position of the Japanese commercial banks is central to their role of designing and implementing the strategic plans of their *keiretsu* groups, especially through their ability to ration credit and control interest rates within their groups. If, for example, Toyota wants a loan, it will get a better interest rate than will other members of the Mitsui group, to which it belongs. The reason is that Toyota is the most internationally-oriented member of the group, and therefore needs the benefit of the lower cost of capital. Other members of the group have, in effect, to bear the cost of this implicit interest subsidy. It is largely the main bank at the core of each group which decides who should get this advantage, based on the recipient's strategic importance to the overall group.

The willingness of the commercial banks to lend very large amounts to corporate borrowers has been facilitated by the Bank of Japan, which allows Japanese banks to have exceedingly high loan-out ratios (often in excess of 1:1) through "overloans." Confronted during much of the postwar period with a demand for funds which they have not been able to satisfy from their deposits, the commercial banks have had heavy recourse to nondeposit sources of funds, such as the rediscount window of the Bank of Japan and the call money market in which other financial institutions place their surplus funds. The major commercial banks have remained in almost constant debt to the central bank. Whereas such a chronic overloan position of commercial banks would seem financially precarious in other countries, the Bank of Japan has made it clear in word and deed that it stands fully behind the banks, and the major commercial banks know that they can rely on the central bank to tide them over any liquidity crisis. Thus, ultimately, there is the Government of Japan in a highly involved role.

The Nature of Financial Risk

In the context of these unique interrelationships among companies, banks and government, several observations central to a foreigner's understanding of corporate financial risk in Japan may be summarized:

1. **The individual company cannot be viewed realistically as an independent financial entity in Japan as it can in, say, the U.S.**

The intimate relationships between companies and banks, and among companies of the same industrial group, enable Japanese firms to safely maintain financial structures that would be almost impossibly risky in an isolated firm. In case of temporary financial adversity, the Japanese company can rely usually on help from other institutions. The lead bank may help directly, and it can help indirectly by arranging loans from other banks. Firms that are customers or suppliers within the group can help by promoting sales of the product, by paying their bills more promptly or by postponing their demands for payment, by discriminatory pricing, or even by providing management assistance. While the Japanese company may be independent in a legal sense, its financial risk situation is more closely akin to a corporate division of a highly diversified conglomerate. The financial strength of the company may be evaluated realistically only in the context of its position in the larger industrial group.

2. **Much of what Americans and Europeans would consider equity risk is borne by the commercial banks in Japan.**

Generally, one of the usually numerous banks from which large Japanese corporations borrow is regarded as the "main" bank. A company entering into a main bank relationship yields an extraordinary amount of power to the bank. The bank, in effect, exercises a tacit veto power over the financial decisions of the firm. It may also inject its executives directly into the senior management of the firm.

In return, the main bank assumes an even greater responsibility than the others with respect to the borrower. The bank, in effect, guarantees the long-term viability of the company by continuing to provide financing in times of adversity or even, in extreme situations, by engineering a merger or takeover by another firm. In the unusual event of a bank-supported firm being forced into default or bankruptcy, other creditors can expect their claims to effectively though not legally outrank those of the main bank. From the perspective of an outside creditor, bankruptcy risk in a Japanese company with main-bank support is almost nonexistent. In a notable example, Kojin Corporation went into bankruptcy several years *after* its main bank relationship with Dai-Ichi Kangyo Bank had deteriorated. Nevertheless, since Kojin had borrowed widely while a full main-bank relationship *had* existed, Dai-Ichi Kangyo undertook voluntarily to repay Kojin's other creditors and absorb the losses itself, thus fulfilling the implicit obligations of main-bank support and avoiding damage to the bank's prestige. A contrasting example is provided by Osawa & Co., the eighth-largest Japanese trading company before its collapse in 1984. A family-owned firm without any group affiliation or main-bank relationship, 82% of its credit was supplied by foreign banks, who suffered major losses from the bankruptcy. It is interesting to speculate whether the foreign banks would have lent so readily to Osawa if they had realized—as the Japanese banks clearly did—that this company really *was* independent, and therefore not subject to the implicit support of a group or a main bank.

3. The nature of debt and equity is different in Japan than elsewhere.

Debt in Japan contains many characteristics that foreigners commonly associate with equity: credit, in the form of bank loans, provides the major financial base of the firm; creditors have a flexible-return obligation in that banks allow their corporate customers to defer interest and principal payments and to reduce compensating balances during financial adversity; the time horizon of the creditors' involvement with the company is infinite, as loans are invariably rolled over; and the creditors, especially the main bank, may actively influence management policy by exercising an implicit veto power over financial decisions or by direct participation in the firm's management.

Common stock, on the other hand, possesses many characteristics that foreigners associate with credit: the stockholders provide a relatively small portion of the firm's total financing; they hold a reasonably fixed return

41

obligation, as dividend payout is traditionally a fixed percentage of the par value of the stock and is rarely changed; and the stockholders usually exercise negligible influences on management. It was suggested by one Japanese securities analyst that foreigners will get a more realistic picture of a Japanese company's financial position by reversing the labels: calling equity debt, and debt equity. While exaggerated, this suggestion nevertheless underscores the importance of the foreigner understanding that characteristics of debt and equity are far more intermingled in Japan than they are elsewhere.

Given these conditions, bankruptcy risk in large Japanese companies is certainly much lower than traditional western accounting measures suggest. The disgrace of financial failure is very much greater in Japan than in America. The traditional method of minimizing this risk has been through a very close (and costly) relationship with one main bank and not, as in a more market-oriented system, by greater recourse to equity.

Empirical testing of financially-troubled Japanese firms by one of the present authors (1) confirms that the true riskiness of a Japanese company is ultimately determined far more by its social importance and the strength of its main bank relationships than by financial conditions reflected in its published financial statements. The tests reveal that risk-measurement standards commonly applied in North America and Western Europe, such as return on investment, debt/equity ratios, cash-flow-coverage ratios, and interest-coverage ratios are of little use in forecasting which financially-troubled Japanese companies will go bankrupt and which will not. By contrast, measures of a firm's social importance (sales volume; number of employees), and of the strength of its main-bank relationship (size of the main bank's loans; share of main-bank holdings of the company's common stock; existence of main-bank personnel in senior management of the company; etc.) are much more reliable indicators of its true bankruptcy risk. Given the pervasive strength of the economic-interest group relations in Japan, our western concepts of assessing the financial soundness of a company as an individual entity, based on data from its financial statements, is largely meaningless in Japan.

Valuation of Equities

Foreigners are also awed and perplexed by what seems—through western eyes—to be the irrational performance of equity markets in Japan, particularly by what is referred to as "the dividend illusion." Western academic models of corporate finance postulate the share value of common stock to equal the total net present value of the expected future stream of dividend flows. By this reasoning, nearly all Japanese equities are grossly overpriced and in imminent danger of collapse. Is this really the case? Once again, western precepts applied to Japan can lead to wildly misleading conclusions.

For a start, capital gains in the hands of most shareholders (including individuals) are not taxed in Japan. Hence Japanese shareholders are happy to see capital gain rather than dividend income. And that is what they get. Dividend payouts in Japan are notoriously low. Dividend yields (dividends as a percentage of the market value of the shares) are around 0.8% in Japan, compared with 3.5% in the U.S. and 4% in Britain. (2)

Nevertheless, Japanese shareholders do well in terms of total returns (see Figure 3-4). In their recent book *Kaisha: The Japanese Corporation,* James Abegglen and George Stalk, two Americans who have spent many years in Japan observing Japanese industry, describe a study of American and Japanese market leaders in 21 different industries. Over the ten years to 1983, Japanese shareholders got a better return than their American counterparts in 16 of the 21 industries. (3) On average, dividends accounted for only 11% of the return to Japanese shareholders but 85% of the return to American shareholders. As Abegglen and Stalk point out, it is hugely inefficient for American companies to pay so much in dividends, as it is equivalent to saying that the shareholder can invest the dividends he receives after tax more productively than the company in which he has invested (presumably on the basis of his belief in its potential growth) can reinvest them (before tax) in itself.

This is at the heart of a significant difference of attitude toward equity between the two countries. *The Economist* sums it up thusly:

> Strange as it may sound, the Japanese have a healthier attitude than market-savvy America. In Japan, equity is still a gamble: the market which provides equity must look mostly to itself (and not to the corporation) for its reward... In America, equity has become too much like debt, with dividends like some sort of debt-servicing payment and quarterly reports to shareholders like progress reports to short-term lenders. As a result, the junk-bond market has become the place to gamble. The more American equity looks like debt without the tax breaks, the more ridiculous it is. (4)

Some of these conditions are, of course, changing in Japan. The internationalization of equity markets is increasing the number of foreign investors in Japanese companies, and they bring with them western views of share ownership. Moreover, ownership is changing within Japan itself, particularly as banks are being forced to reduce their shareholdings in individual companies to 5% or less by December 1987. Nevertheless, the overriding differences remain: that American managers place their main emphasis on the return on investment—a shareholder-driven financial

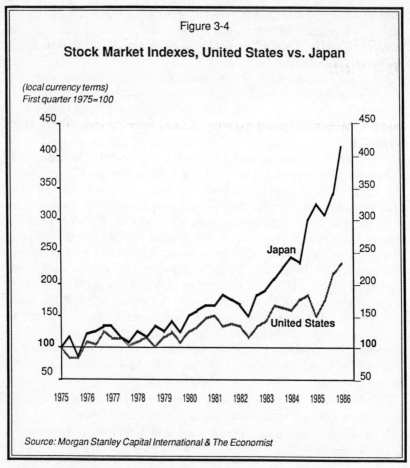

Figure 3-4

Stock Market Indexes, United States vs. Japan

(local currency terms)
First quarter 1975=100

Source: Morgan Stanley Capital International & The Economist

objective—while Japanese management's top priority is gaining market share—a business objective. Foreigners who fail to fully appreciate that distinction are likely to draw wildly unrealistic conclusions about the objectives and performance of Japanese finance.

1. Richard W. Wright and Sadahiko Suzuki, "Financial Structure and Bankruptcy Risk in Japanese Companies," *Journal of International Business Studies,* Spring 1985, pp. 97-110.
2. "Equity: The Last Resort," *The Economist,* June 7, 1986, p. 34.
3. James C. Abegglen and George Stalk, Jr., *Kaisha, The Japanese Corporation* (New York: Basic Books, 1985), p. 168.
4. *The Economist,* op. cit., p. 34.

CHAPTER 4

Capital Exports: The Japanese Money Machine

Japan is the world's largest exporter of cash, eclipsing even OPEC at its heyday.

Armed with a population of some 115 million people devoted to the work ethic to an extent unparalleled elsewhere, an intelligent, co-operative government-industry relationship, a firm grasp of marketing, an extraordinarily high savings rate, and a national policy of promoting export-led growth, Japan has soared from the status of financial weakling to that of financial superpower, with an average per-capita income now exceeding even that of the United States.(1)

Japan's enormous capital surplus position has grown at an astonishing rate. Figure 4-1 illustrates the development of Japan's economy from that of net capital importer in the early sixties to the recent phenomenon of wholesale capital exporter. What OPEC achieved over a century through the role of supplier of the main fuel of the world's growth, Japan has achieve in less than thirty years—from the rubble of a defeated nation, with no indigenous resources, as a small island at the other end of the economic world. Furthermore, the Japanese have shown an ability both to target certain industrial sectors and to change those targets as their comparative advantages shift, as OPEC attempted but did not entirely succeed in doing, thus eliminating over-reliance on any one sector for economic growth.

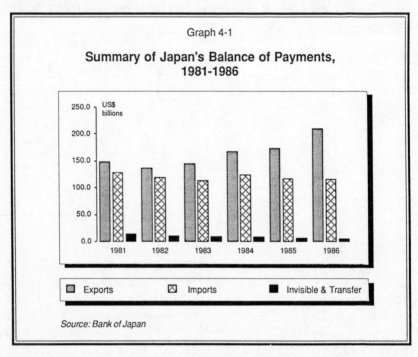

Graph 4-1

Summary of Japan's Balance of Payments, 1981-1986

Source: Bank of Japan

As there are few signs of any significant long-term faltering in the Japanese economy, Japanese capital exports are almost certain to continue unabated for the foreseeable future. And unlike OPEC, which was content to recycle its trade surpluses through foreign banks, the Japanese are determined that it should be *their* financial institutions which control the dispersion of these funds—a development which will have profound effects on financial centres and financial institutions throughout the world.

Genesis

Explaining the recent phenomenon of massive Japanese capital exports requires firstly an understanding of the extraordinarily high savings rate in Japan. At 17% of disposable income, the Japanese savings rate is the highest in the world, over four times that of the U.S. (See Figure 4-2 for comparative data.) Undoubtedly, Japanese culture plays a major part in this eagerness to save. The Confucianist ethic of thriftiness underlies the Japanese way of life. And centuries of survival on severely crowded islands with few natural means of support have taught the Japanese to sacrifice or defer personal pleasure in the form of a higher standard of living in order to benefit the larger group, be it the family, the company, or the country.

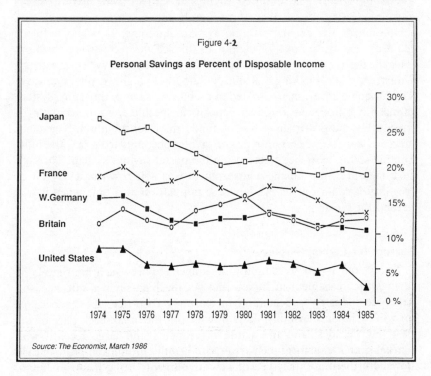

Figure 4-2

Personal Savings as Percent of Disposable Income

Source: The Economist, March 1986

Other significant causes of the Japanese' savings habit include the importance that the Japanese attach to education, and the lack of adequate retirement pensions. As a culture, the Japanese place a very high emphasis on the education of their children. From an early age, Japanese children spend countless "free" hours in private tutorials and special classes designed to supplement their basic education. This amounts to years of additional intense studying far beyond that which is required in any western country. Parents must save in order to finance this as well as post-secondary education.

47

Furthermore, the lack of adequate public pension schemes forces Japanese wage-earners to put away a significant portion of their earnings to provide for retirement. The Japanese have the fastest ageing population in the world, and the inadequate public pension programs necessitate the accumulation by individuals of large sums of money for comfortable retirements, the cumulative effect of which represents a massive hording of capital.

Finally, government-imposed savings incentives were used to great advantage after World War II to supply the funds necessary for the rebuilding of the Japanese economy. At that time, Japanese industry required massive inflows of capital to finance the reconstruction effort after the destruction brought about by the war. Such heavy "smokestack" industries as steel-making and ship-building were highly capital intensive. The Japanese government assisted in mobilizing savings through a system of incentives designed to render deposits in specific types of accounts an irresistably more attractive use of funds than consumption. The main measure was to free certain types of savings accounts from tax, the most notable still in existence today being the postal savings system. Through such measures, the Japanese government was able to wring every bit of frugality it could out of the Japanese population at a time when it was needed the most.

Reasons for Capital Surplus

Today, the Japanese economy no longer requires such high levels of savings for investment in Japan, and yet the high savings rate persists. Japanese industry is becoming increasingly cash-rich, as the pace of growth in Japan inevitably slows down from the break-neck pace of the past few decades, and the astute investments and large recently-won market shares transform themselves into healthy profits and positive cash flows. Furthermore, the type of new investments being made in Japan, although still substantial in size, cannot compare in capital requirements to the heavy industries of the 1950s and 60s. Accordingly, as Japanese high savings rates persist, the coffers of the nation are beginning to overflow. For example, the previously-mentioned Japanese postal savings system has grown into a financial organism of truly mammoth proportions: deposits accumulated through its some 23,000 postal outlets equal over U.S. $600 billion,(2) making it by far the largest body of savings in the world, greater than the four largest commercial banks in Japan combined.

Today Japan is a rich country, with an average per-capita income equal to $17,000 U.S. (versus $16,000 in the United States).(3) There are some indications that a younger generation of Japanese are becoming more inclined to enjoy some of the fruits of their labors than the "old guard" now in place, and as Japan begins to relent and open itself up more and more to outside influences and lifestyles, this trend will continue. Nevertheless, the savings rate in Japan should remain well above world norms for the foreseeable future, thus continuing the Japanese accumulation of larger and larger mountains of cash.

A separate but related factor is the ever-increasing Japanese trade surplus. Figure 4-3 shows the Japanese current account balance for the years 1974-85. It is notable that even after the oil shocks of 1973 and 1979, the Japanese economy recovered quickly to very solid current account surpluses. A near-mirror image of the current account balance is the net

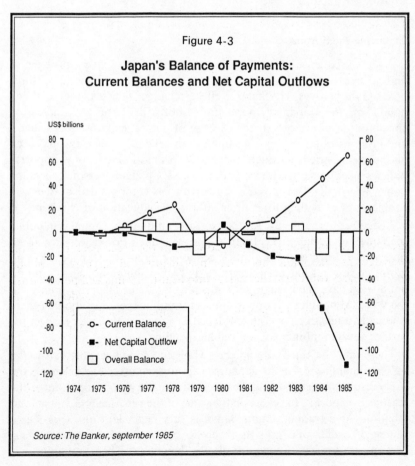

Figure 4-3

Japan's Balance of Payments:
Current Balances and Net Capital Outflows

US$ billions

Legend:
-O- Current Balance
-■- Net Capital Outflow
□ Overall Balance

Source: The Banker, september 1985

capital outflow superimposed on the same graph (Figure 4-3). It is not at all unusual that an island nation such as Japan has emerged as heavily dependent on exports. As a country with few natural resources save an educated, thrifty population, Japan's economic survival depends to a large extent on its ability to import raw materials and semi-finished products, perform high value-added operations, and export the finished products. The Japanese have been particularly astute at promoting exports while at the same time inhibiting imports through barriers to entry or through nationalistic behaviour on the part of the Japanese consumer. The large volume of trade which is transacted in non-yen currencies has become an enormous source of foreign capital which must sooner or later be used either to purchase imports, or to buy assets abroad such as foreign securities or factories.

Exporting the Surplus

As a consequence of all these forces, the Japanese have a problem in finding a profitable home for their cash. They have, basically, three possible alternatives. The first is to effect a change in the personal spending habits of the Japanese population, both in terms of increasing consumption of imports at the expense of domestically produced items, and in terms of increasing consumption in general. In fact, this has been halfheartedly tried, through the active promotion of "buy imports" policies by politicians, with very little success. Changing personal spending habits is a difficult proposal at best, which is compounded by the twin problems of providing for retirement and the education of children.

A second alternative use for the excessive amounts of capital is in public spending on social infrastructure and the like. Foreigners are often surprised to learn that for all their economic might, the Japanese live all too often in what has been described as "rabbit-hutch housing," and do not always have the basic water and sewage systems taken for granted in the West. Although such opportunities for public spending abound, there is already a massive government deficit in Japan, with little prospect for further substantial increases in public spending.

Therefore, the third alternative—wholesale capital exporting—is the only remaining use for the Japanese capital surpluses. Furthermore, the likely results of *not* exporting the excess capital are just as important as the reasons *to* export it: the effect on the value of the yen, unemployment, and inflation. As a trading nation, Japan is very dependent on exports as a source of profits and growth. A cheap or under-valued currency is a prerequisite for healthy exports. If the Japanese wished to retain their capital surpluses in Japan for use at home, it would require the exchange (sale) of export-earned dollars into yen. The result would be a decrease in demand for dollars and an increase in demand for yen, causing the value of the yen to rise, with the resultant loss of the cost advantages of many Japanese exports. Industrial output and growth would fall as the loss of exports caused a ripple effect throughout the economy, with attendant unemployment and hardship, especially in the small-business and sub-contracting sectors. The increased surplus of yen would also expand the Japanese money supply and likely increase the rate of inflation. Accordingly, having recognized the necessity of exporting capital, the Japanese, in characteristic fashion, are pursuing that objective with a vengeance.

Exodus

As sources of capital in Japan have risen inexorably over the past decade while opportunities for investment in Japan have dwindled, the stream of capital to the West has become a tidal wave, with $81 billion of Japanese long-term capital flowing overseas in 1985, and an astonishing $180 billion estimated for 1986. (See Graph 4-4.)

In making their overseas investments, the Japanese are characteristically low risk takers, both in terms of the location of investment and in terms of its form. Accordingly, only countries with the highest ratings of creditworthiness have been chosen as suitable for investment. The United States has accounted for by far the majority of the investment, with most of the remainder going to the other traditionally stable countries of Canada, Australia and the European Community. It is interesting to note that the Japanese have largely avoided the pitfalls of Third World lending that have plagued so many western bankers in the past. In the late 1970s, a few Japanese banks took large losses on loans to Iran and Latin America, and it is apparent that the Japanese have learned their lesson well and now view security as a critical factor in making their international investment decisions. This policy of avoiding loan default at all costs is perhaps due to Japanese fear of jeopardizing pension assets, and explains why American and other foreign securities are gobbled up even with the prospect of continued devaluation of the dollar.

The form of investment abroad exemplifies the Japanese low-risk policy and penchant for highly liquid securities such as bonds or publicly-traded shares. In 1985, some $54 billion of the total $81 billion invested abroad was in the form of U.S. Treasury bonds. The massive Japanese purchases of Treasury bonds have in fact been financing the U.S. budget deficit, with

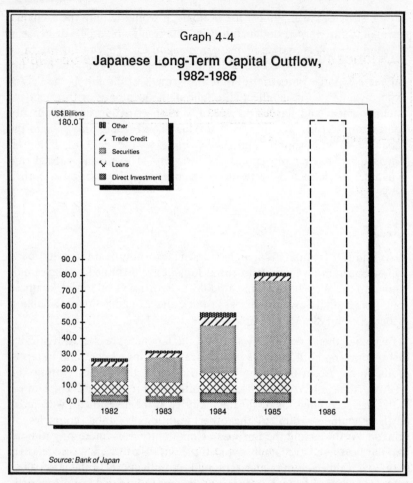

Graph 4-4

Japanese Long-Term Capital Outflow, 1982-1986

US$ Billions

Legend:
- Other
- Trade Credit
- Securities
- Loans
- Direct Investment

Source: Bank of Japan

some unsettling implications. Given the high liquidity and short-term nature of the securities, it would not be difficult for the Japanese to withdraw their funds on relatively short notice, with a corresponding shock to the American financial system (much the same as in the "rollover" syndrome feared during the heyday of the OPEC cartel).

Table 4-5 illustrates the preponderance of bonds over stocks in Japanese foreign securities investments. When the Japanese do invest in equity at all, they have shown a distinct preference for portfolio ownership of equity in foreign firms over direct investment, apparently reasoning that it is preferable to own the stock of a foreign firm than to make an investment in concrete and steel.

Table 4-5

Japanese Long-Term Capital Outflows, 1982-1986
(US$ billions)

	1982	1983	1984	1985	1986
Direct Investment	4.5	3.6	6.0	6.5	
Loans	7.9	8.4	11.9	10.6	
Securities					
Bonds	6.1	12.5	26.8	53.5	
Samurai's, etc.	3.5	2.9	4.0	5.3	
Stocks	0.2	0.7	0.1	1.0	
Trade Credit	3.2	2.6	4.9	3.0	
Other	2.0	1.8	3.2	2.3	
	27.4	**32.5**	**56.8**	**82.2**	**180.0** (projected)

Source: Bank of Japan

There is evidence that equity will become a more common form of investment abroad by Japanese investors. One argument for such a shift is that, as the financial markets and consumers in Japan become increasingly sophisticated, Japanese individuals will be able to get, and will demand, higher returns than the very low yields (currently 2-3%) available on government-encouraged domestic deposits. In particular, Japanese appear increasingly to recognize that by focusing their overseas investments so heavily into non-equity securities, they are really short-changing themselves out of higher potential returns, as Japanese-owned funds are used by foreigners for projects and investments which produce higher returns for them than the interest rates they have to pay the Japanese. Thus foreign producers are able to boost their production levels and market share, while the Japanese earn their relatively low interest. Political pressures from Japan's trading partners are also forcing more Japanese investors into direct investment positions (see Figure 4-6).

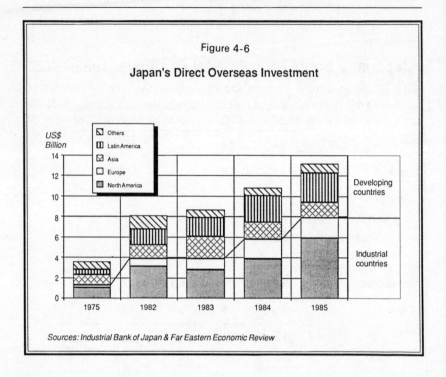

Figure 4-6

Japan's Direct Overseas Investment

Sources: *Industrial Bank of Japan & Far Eastern Economic Review*

Impact

The first impact that this vast outpouring of capital will have is on the financial landscape of the world. Tokyo is already becoming the third leg of the New York–London network required to create a truly international, 24-hour financial market, superceding the roles of the other major Southeast Asian centres of Hong Kong and Singapore. Foreign financial institutions will continue to open up offices in Tokyo in an attempt to handle some of that flow of funds. Tokyo will meet all the requirements of a world-class financial centre: a large domestic economy, an internationalized currency, the basic institutional framework, skilled personnel, and a sufficiently liberalized environment to allow and encourage the type of risk-taking, innovation, and attendant rewards that provide the incentive for financial institutions to take a stake in a financial centre.

A second major effect of the capital exports will be on Japanese financial institutions. As Tokyo develops into a world-class financial centre, it will be Japanese financial institutions which, as the natural collectors and disbursors of the Japanese capital surplus, will most benefit. The large amounts of funds available to them will always leave them one step ahead of their western peers, as they embark on a path that will lead them to control those funds at all stages (see Chapter 8).

To put it in different terms, the Japanese now have a comparative advantage in a commodity even more important than oil: money. And that advantage will be exploited for all its worth to advance the cause of the latest wave of Japanese commercial warriors: the Japanese banks and securities companies.

1 "Richer than You," *The Economist,* October 25, 1986, pp.13-14.
2 "Japanese Post Offices Awash with Lolly," *Asia Banking,* February 1986, p.50.
3 *The Economist,* op. cit.

CHAPTER 5

Japanese Banks: Financial Juggernauts

The five largest banks in the world are Japanese

The Japanese have infiltrated the ranks of the world's biggest banks, an area which many thought would always be the exclusive domain of the Americans and the Europeans. This has all come about in an extraordinarily quick fashion. As recently as 1980 none of Japan's banks ranked among the world's top five in size of deposits, and only one (Dai-Ichi Kangyo) ranked among the first ten. Today the top five are all Japanese, and thirteen Japanese banks rank among the largest 25 (see Figure 5-1). Tokyo-based Dai-Ichi Kangyo toppled Citicorp in 1985 as the world's largest commercial banking concern, tipping the scales at a hefty $207

billion in first-quarter 1986 assets (compared with Citicorp's $176 billion), up from only $17 billion in 1971—an average compound growth rate of over 16%. And the trend is likely to accelerate even more as the Japanese consolidate their control over large sectors of the world's banking industry. Moreover, as the yen eventually succumbs to pressures forcing it to rise further against most other currencies, most notably the U.S. dollar, the relative size of the Japanese banks will jump even further, with perhaps twenty-five of them counted in the ranks of the world's top fifty.

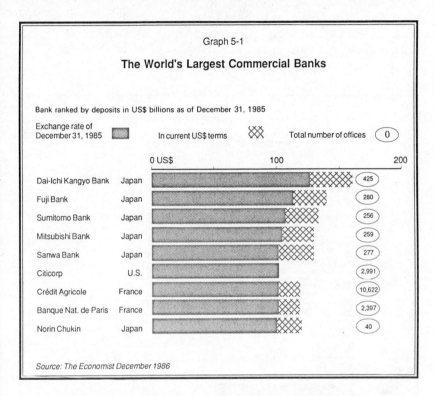

Graph 5-1

The World's Largest Commercial Banks

Bank ranked by deposits in US$ billions as of December 31, 1985

| Exchange rate of December 31, 1985 | | In current US$ terms | | Total number of offices | |

Growth in size is only one part of the latest Japanese success story. Japanese banks are beginning to export cash in much the same way as Toyota exported cars. In 1985 Japan's banks overtook their U.S. counterparts as the world's largest international lenders, with $650 billion in loans outstanding, compared with $600 billion for American institutions. (1) By September 1986 Japanese banks held nearly 32% of the total worldwide assets of banks (see Figure 5-2). And their dominance in international lending shows no signs of abating. A report issued recently by Nomura Securities Co. predicts that by 1995 Japan will have an astonishing *$1 trillion* in loans outstanding. (2) The Japanese are now the largest force in foreign banking in the U.S., with 5.8% of total U.S. banking assets (45% of the foreign sector's share) and the second largest in London, with 23% of total U.K. banking assets (3). (By way of comparison, *total* foreign

TSW–E

banking assets in Japan account for less than 3% of the Japanese loan market!) Japanese banks have picked up major chunks of American and European commercial lending, particularly where low interest rates are more important than innovation. Recently freed from some of the restrictions of the tightly-controlled Japanese domestic market, Japanese banks abroad are also engaging in new activities such as trust banking and securities underwriting, threatening the domain of both Japanese and foreign securities firms.

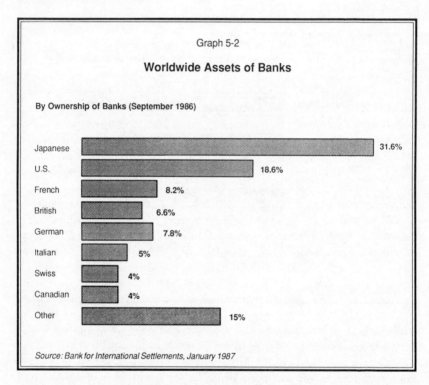

Graph 5-2

Worldwide Assets of Banks

By Ownership of Banks (September 1986)

Japanese	31.6%
U.S.	18.6%
French	8.2%
British	6.6%
German	7.8%
Italian	5%
Swiss	4%
Canadian	4%
Other	15%

Source: Bank for International Settlements, January 1987

How and why has all this come about? What are Japanese banks doing that their western counterparts aren't—or can't? Are western banks doomed to endure the same difficulties already experienced by automotive and consumer electronics industries? It is impossible to predict the exact route which Japanese banks will chart in the next decade, but it is generally conceded that a nation's banks cannot be successful without a strong, successful economy behind them powering the banks' growth. And the Japanese have the slickest, best controlled, most vigorous economy in the world, and lots and lots of cash.

From little acorns...

Japanese corporations have a history of debt financing to the exclusion of other forms of financing, to the benefit of Japanese banks. The most common form of this lending is short-term notes or loans which are continually rolled over to become a virtually permanent source of capital. This attachment to loans was due in part to historic underdevelopment of the stock market, limits on the price of new equity issues, and tax legislation which favored debt over equity financing (see Chapter 3). The debt-to-equity ratios of Japanese firms in the 1970s averaged 2:1, whereas the equivalent numbers in the U.S. were 0.5:1. This inclination towards continuous debt financing stood Japanese commercial banks in good stead during the post-war rebuilding and growth years and provided the base for their growth.

However, all that is changing now, and banks are finding themselves in an entirely different set of circumstances. For one thing, the Japanese economy is slowing down, with growth rates of 4–5%, down from the 8% average growth rates of the 1960s and 70s. This slowing down in growth translates into lower loan demand from Japanese corporations. With slower growth, Japanese corporations are not being required to invest as much money in basic infrastructure facilities such as factories and equipment, and are increasingly turning into cash cows which provide a steady stream of profits from the large market shares won during the last decade. At least 20 Japanese companies now report surplus cash reserves of more than $2 billion each. Toyota Motors leads with $12.5 billion in cash and marketable securities, followed by Matsushita ($9.4 billion), Hitachi ($6.2 billion), and Sanyo ($2.8 billion).(4) Thus, instead of being in chronic need of cash to keep up with expansion, Japanese companies are accumulating cash surpluses which give their bankers the mixed blessing of vast amounts of available cash, but fewer and fewer opportunities to put it to work in Japan.

Compounding the problem for the Japanese banks is the ever-increasing sophistication and ability of corporations to find other sources of capital, either in Japan or overseas:

> In Japan, the big corporations, many of them flush with funds, are shunning traditional financing and investment techniques and making increasing use of international markets. Relationships with main banks are shifting and loyalties diminishing. It is very difficult now for a company to ignore the possibility of raising funds in the international markets as an alternative to raising funds in Japan.(5)

Not only that, the traditional territory of the banks both inside and outside of Japan is being encroached upon by aggressive Japanese securities houses. In the wake of a growing wave of deregulation, the securities firms are doing particularly well both at taking away sources of low-cost deposits from banks by offering higher-yielding money market and other securities-based funds, and in finding underwriting clients to take the excess cash.

The net result is that Japanese banks are facing a dwindling lending market in Japan, and as the demand for loans falls, so does the price. A first consequence is that bank margins in Japan are now among the lowest in the world (typically 0.125–0.375%). For some foreign banks, this has meant that breaking into the Japanese loan market, an extraordinarily trying task in the best of times, has become almost impossible. Some foreign banks with their backs up against the wall have tried to beat the miserly spreads by lending to the disreputable Japanese *sarakin,* or loan sharks. Others, like American Express in 1985, have given up on the traditional lending business altogether and moved into the securities business in Japan. Though they may not be in such dire straits, the Japanese banks too are casting their gaze about for new markets to lift them from their current malaise.

A related effect of the new cash abundance of Japanese companies is a slow but steady decline in the central coordinating and strategic role of the banks within their *keiretsu* groups, as member companies stray from their traditional banking relationships. The combination of shrinking profit margins and eroding economic clout at home leaves Japan's banks only one real avenue for growth: international expansion.

Blueprint for Success

Having discovered that expansion into overseas markets is essentially their only option for growth, Japanese banks use characteristically Japanese marketing tactics which are already very familiar to other western industries which have had the misfortune to feel their sting. First off, they make full use of the strong tendencies of Japanese corporations to stick to doing business with other Japanese corporations with which they are familiar. Such strong ties often carry over to the West, where, to gain a toehold into a new market, Japanese banks will first begin by following loyal Japanese clients which are establishing manufacturing operations in an area, thereby maintaining their traditional business ties. In much the same way that American banks followed American multinationals over to Europe in the 1950s and 60s, Japanese banks are poised to follow their traditional benefactors, to the dismay of potential non-Japanese competitors:

A banker from Atlanta tells the story of how he saw Japanese companies setting up all over his territory and was delighted at the new business apparently flowing his way. However, his hopes of prosperity were short-lived as Japanese banks suddenly established branches in the region and snapped up all the business overnight. Such strong links are very hard to break. (6)

After becoming thus firmly established, the Japanese use what has always been their marketing trademark to gain market share: low prices. We are all familiar with how the Japanese began to sell cars at prices that American automakers could not match; and the battle over Japanese predatory pricing of silicon chips in the U.S. market, though temporarily on hold as the result of the controversial bilateral governmental chip deal, is far from settled (see Chapter 8). The Japanese are doing precisely the same thing in world loan markets: offering loans at margins that have been cut to the bone. As one example, Mitsubishi Bank beat out its American competitors with an aggressive bid for a recent $500 million loan to NWA Inc., the parent of Northwest Airlines, to finance the purchase of Republic Airlines. An executive of an American bank that lost out on the bid summed it up simply: "They beat us on price." (7)

By undercutting competitors on price, the Japanese have been able to take large chunks of business away from western bankers. Nowhere is this more evident than in loans to governments. The Japanese have become clear leaders in government lending, by offering interest rates often only $\frac{1}{16}$ of 1% over cost. If we add to this their cheaper access to funds in the first place, it is no surprise that as early as 1982 we began hearing cries from western bankers that "the Japanese are dumping financial services!" But few western governments have been in a mood to try to curb the flow, as Japanese largesse offers them a reliable, cut-rate means of sustaining their own fiscal deficits.

Of course, the first thought that comes to mind is that if the Japanese want to provide loans at extremely low margins, let them go ahead, because American and European clients will gain cheap financing which they can invest to produce higher returns, and Japanese banks will lose their shirts in the bargain. The first conclusion is true, but the second takes a very shortsighted view at best, and at worst represents the kind of complacent attitude which spelled the demise of western consumer electronics and motorcycle industries. It is undeniable that the low-priced, high-quality Japanese consumer products with which we are all so familiar are a boon to the populations of western nations, but the effects of the overly-aggressive Japanese pricing is less benign for the western corporations trying to offer those same products. The Japanese take a very long-term view of profitability, and accordingly are quite willing to sacrifice short-term profits in order to gain long-term market share. Numerous studies have indicated that high market shares lead inexorably to higher profits, as increasing economies of scale eventually catch up to the lower prices. And in the meantime, those competitors who are unable or unwilling to enter into the fray find themselves with dwindling market shares and resources *and* lower profitability.

What is required for such a strategy to succeed is a vast reservoir of resources behind the price-cutting institutions, and an inability on the part of the competition to fight in the same manner. In financial services, the Japanese have both. Japan's continual capital and trade surpluses provide Japanese banks with ample supplies of cash to feed to their front lines, while western institutions are effectively prevented by Japanese government regulations and cultural attitudes from getting access to the same cheap Japanese deposits available to Japanese banks. The ability of western financial houses to engage in bare-bones price-cutting competition is further constrained by their need to provide sustained dividend flows to shareholders with relatively short-term profit horizons, as explained in Chapter 3.

Learning from Others

Many western bankers feel that the Japanese still lag behind in certain areas such as fund management, and in their general ability to engineer innovative financial packages involving, for example, complex swap arrangements. It is true that the stifled and highly segregated Japanese domestic market has resulted in little past innovation; in fact it is widely suggested that this is the cause of the slow deregulation efforts of Japanese authorities: to allow Japanese banks, through a little controlled shoulder-rubbing with slick western bankers, to be brought up to international standards. But when the Japanese know that they are behind in something, they *always* study, study, study, until they've mastered their former deficiency. Or they headhunt for a western executive who has already done the studying for them. Traditionally far less generous to their employees than comparable western firms, Japanese banks (and other financial institutions) are beginning to fork out the kind of money required to entice foreign executives to jump ship (see Chapter 2). Moreover, the strong attachment of Japanese employees to their company, and their unwillingness to break the very real social and cultural bonds that tie them to their organizations, make it unlikely that Japanese banks will ever experience the same erosion of their staff they are able to inflict upon their competition.

Without a doubt, however, the joint venture with a western financial institution has become the favorite Japanese tactic of gaining access to skills and information. In some cases, Japanese government regulations on foreign activities in Japan virtually force the foreigners into joint ventures. A case in point is the opening up of the Japanese trust banking (pension fund) market to foreigners in 1985. The rules governing the foreign bankers' operations stipulated, among other things, that:

> The applicant must be engaged in trust business in its home country; . . .
> The applicant is required to employ staff knowledgeable of Japanese trust business, particularly pension fund business. (8)

In other words, "We only want you if your are experienced in what you do, and you are going to have to either form a joint-venture with a Japanese firm, or hire away their employees." Not surprisingly then, eight of the nine foreign applications for trust banking licenses involved joint ventures with Japanese firms. The end result will likely be marginal or unprofitable operations for the foreign firms, and increased skills and expertise, at little additional cost, for the Japanese partners. (Decontrol of the Japanese financial markets is discussed further in Chapter 7.)

The willingness of Japanese banks to lend their employees to new foreign financial institutions does not spring from a genuine heartfelt desire to lend an encouraging hand; rather, it provides the Japanese with a complete view of the foreigner's operations while shielding their own activities from view. For the Japanese, rather than "You show me, and I'll show you," it's "You show me, and I'll show my boss!" Foreign bankers in Tokyo claim that this is precisely how the Japanese have acquired, in the short span of a couple of years, their market position in foreign exchange dealing.

Branching Out

Overseas, Japanese firms engage in joint ventures with or outright acquisitions of foreign financial institutions to gain expertise, to obtain access to branch networks and contacts, and to avoid certain limitations on foreign bank activities. In 1984, for example, Sumitomo Bank bought a 52% controlling interest in the Swiss bank, Banca del Gottardo, to become the largest foreign bank in that country, with direct access to large-scale European trust banking. In Britain, the Bank of Tokyo formed a joint venture with the investment company, Touche Remnant, to acquire expertise on funds management. In the U.S., one of the favorite haunts of the Japanese Banks has been California, where, for example, Mitsubishi

Bank acquired Bank of California and Bank of Tokyo acquired California First Bank. Japan's banks seem increasingly willing overseas to abandon the traditional Japanese distaste for takeovers, by acquiring financially-troubled western banks or, in some cases, even initiating hostile takeovers.

By buying out an American or other foreign bank, the Japanese banks can get a ready-made clientele and distribution system, something that foreign banks are again legally prevented from doing in Japan by administrative obfuscation. Rumors are, for example, that when Citicorp seemed interested in buying out the financially-troubled Heiwa Shogo Bank, the Ministry of Finance engineered a merger with Sumitomo Bank in order to block a foreign entry to the retail banking business in the Land of the Rising Sun.

Through carefully designed joint ventures and acquisitions, Japanese banks have been able to move with great speed into entirely new areas of business where they formerly lacked expertise. These cooperative efforts have exposed them to such new activities as leasing, credit cards, venture capital and factoring, thus opening major new avenues for expansion.

In a recent *Harvard Business Review* article titled "Joint Ventures with Japan Give Away Our Future," Robert Reich and Eric Mankin point astutely to the lop-sided advantages gained by the Japanese in many of these ventures. Though their focus is mainly on manufacturing joint ventures, their conclusions apply equally to financial services:

> On the surface, the arrangements seem fair and well balanced, indicative of an evolving international economic equilibrium. A closer examination, however, shows these deals for what they really are—part of a continuing, implicit Japanese strategy to keep the higher-paying, higher-value added jobs in Japan and to gain the . . . process skills that underlie competitive success. (9)

Examples abound of Japanese banks successfully diversifying through overseas acquisitions or mergers. Sanwa Bank took over the Continental Leasing Corporation and transformed it into Sanwa Business Credit Corporation. The same Sanwa Bank invited Germany's Dresdner Bank to form a joint venture with them in the People's Republic of China, together with the Bank of China, to launch a leasing company called Universal Leasing Company. Mitsubishi Trust Bank also set up a leasing joint venture with Mitsubishi Corporation and Thomas Harrington, the former president of Chemlease. Mitsubishi decided not only to headhunt Harrington; they decided to make him an important minority shareholder as the surest way of avoiding his leaving the venture. Golden State Sanwa Bank, the subsidiary of Sanwa in California with $1.2 billion in assets, is a diversified financial group specialising in leasing, factoring and credit card business. Is it a surprise that the world's fifth-largest credit card is JCB, launched in 1962 by Sanwa in cooperation with American Express? With its 6.2 million cardholders and 20% annual growth rate, JCB plans to double its outlets by 1988 to 60 countries and 50,000 shops and restaurants.

And Still Other Cards to Play

Quality is something that Japanese manufacturers have made famous, and it appears that the Japanese banks are also successfully adapting the concept to financial services. For the Japanese banks, high quality is really nothing more than attention to detail and plain hard work. By ensuring that every part of a transaction has been thoroughly screened and analysed, Japanese banks will eventually earn a reputation of providing trouble-free loans in much the same way as the Japanese manufacturers became recognized for their well-built cars. If a Japanese bank is involved in a swap, for instance, it will assign staff to examine the swap documents in minute detail for possible errors. "They call me up in the evening to point out spelling errors we've made in the English text," said one American banker, who can't be bothered to read the paperwork before he sends it out.(10) This is really just a reflection of the strong Japanese commitment to their company, and a desire to do all that is possible to ensure success, even if it should mean working long into the evening poring over documents.

Finally, a discussion of the Japanese banks' international expansion strategies would not be complete without mentioning Japan's connection with China. Because of the historic relationship between the two countries and their shared cultural values, Japan could very well be the conduit for world access to China as it continues to open its markets to the world. Already, Japanese banks have set up 55 banking offices in China, the largest concentration of Japanese banks anywhere in the world. They are engaged in a wide variety of activities there. As western corporations fall over themselves trying to position themselves for the day when an economy of over a billion industrious people is unleashed upon the world (if that day ever comes), Japan can efficiently act as an intermediary:

> What counts is the Japanese ability to use their presence in China as a marketing tool. Sanwa, for example, has just opened an office in Atlanta, Georgia. Asked how he hoped to get in the door of middle-market corporations in Dixie, Kawakatsu (President of Sanwa Bank) immediately produced the China card. "If customers in Atlanta want business from China, we'll give them no end of information."(11)

Again, it should not be too surprising that in 1985, even in the midst of trade frictions between Japan and China, a consortium of 73 Japanese banks took only three weeks to put together a $2 billion commercial loan to the Chinese government to help secure Japanese trading interests.

Conclusion

Japanese banks are positioned to further dominate many areas of international banking to an extent that would have been unthinkable just a short while ago. The only remaining question is to what extent they will do so, and in what particular areas. Not all of this is necessarily bad for the West. In fact, Japanese capital is helping significantly to fund the deficits of the United States and other western governments, and therefore temporarily propping up our cherished standard of living. Japanese low-cost loans will certainly benefit their recipients, and the Japanese banking invasion will probably deservedly bring about a day of reckoning for many western banks which are inefficient or needlessly backward in their practises. However, the damage may be much greater than that if western banks, as their manufacturing counterparts did, ignore the warning signs until it's too late to recover what were once strongholds of western banking.

1. "Money Masters from the East," *Time,* August 11, 1986, p. 31.
2. "Who's Doing the Business?," *Euromoney,* August 1985, p. 151.
3. "Money Masters," op. cit., p. 32.
4. David Lake, "Cash-Rich Giants Ready for Corporate Raids," *Asian Finance,* August 15, 1986, p. 14.
5. "Are Japan's Banks Losing Out?," *Euromoney,* September 1985, p. 105.
6. Ibid., p. 110.
7. Gary Hector, "The Japanese Want to Be Your Bankers," *Fortune,* October 27, 1986, p. 98.
8. "Paper Tigers in Japan's Trust Market," *Asia Banking,* May 1985, p. 94.
9. Robert B. Reich and Eric D. Mankin, "Joint Ventures with Japan Give Away our Future," *Harvard Business Review*, March-April 1986, p. 78.
10. "Now, the Japanese Attack the World's Financial Markets," *Euromoney,* October 1985, p. 77.
11. Ibid., p. 91.

CHAPTER 6

The Brokers: Elbowing In

Four of the six largest securities houses in the world are Japanese.

Like their banking counterparts, Japanese securities firms are becoming increasingly dominant forces in their international activities. Already, Nomura Securities Company is the largest in the world in terms of assets, bigger even than the American giant Merrill Lynch, and vastly more profitable: Nomura's pre-tax profits for 1986 exceeded $3 billion. So colossal is Nomura that its market capitalization, or what the stock market

says all its shares are worth, is ten times that of Merrill Lynch. (1) In a takeover financed with stock, Nomura could easily swallow Merrill Lynch like a bit of predinner sushi. The "Big Four" Japanese securities firms (Nomura, Nikko, Daiwa and Yamaichi) are all well within the ranks of the world's ten largest securities companies (see Figure 6-1). Together they account for over half of the trading volume on the Tokyo Stock Exchange (TSE). To put that into perspective, the TSE has more volume than *all* of the exchanges of Europe combined; it has just topped even New York as the world's largest exchange, with a market capitalization of $2,740 billion versus New York's $2,580 billion.(2) (Even the comparatively minor Osaka exchange has now passed London to become the world's third largest, after New York and Tokyo.) While Japanese banks are sometimes regarded as plodding, conservative organizations, Japanese securities firms have been extremely aggressive at home and abroad both in increasing their volume of business, and in rapidly innovating into new product areas and encroaching upon the traditional turf of the Japanese commercial banks and other financial institutions.

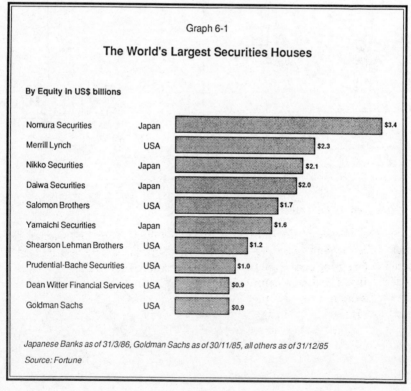

Graph 6-1

The World's Largest Securities Houses

By Equity in US$ billions

Nomura Securities	Japan	$3.4
Merrill Lynch	USA	$2.3
Nikko Securities	Japan	$2.1
Daiwa Securities	Japan	$2.0
Salomon Brothers	USA	$1.7
Yamaichi Securities	Japan	$1.6
Shearson Lehman Brothers	USA	$1.2
Prudential-Bache Securities	USA	$1.0
Dean Witter Financial Services	USA	$0.9
Goldman Sachs	USA	$0.9

Japanese Banks as of 31/3/86, Goldman Sachs as of 30/11/85, all others as of 31/12/85
Source: Fortune

One measure of their success is their profitability. In 1985, Japanese securities firms were the first, fourth, eighth, and tenth most profitable financial institutions in Japan. And their earnings continue to skyrocket: average profits of the Big Four in the accounting year ended September 1986 grew an astonishing 82%, totalling some one trillion yen or $5.4 billion! (See Table 6-2.) In American and European underwritings, Japanese securities firms have become increasingly adept at using their vast financial clout to reduce prices and take inordinately large chunks of new issues back to Japan, where their outstanding placement power enables them to quickly dispose of their holdings. Their immense profitability at home has allowed the securities companies to enter other lucrative markets as they embark on a path that will eventually make them truly financial supermarkets.

Table 6-2

Earnings per share of major Japanese Securities Firms

	Sept. '80	Sept '81	Sept. '82	Sept. '83	Sept. '84	Mar. '85
Nomura	23.7	26.3	20.6	29.5	39.2	49.6
Nikko	19.7	18.8	13.5	18.6	27	37.2
Yamaichi	16.7	18.1	15.5	18.6	29.3	42.6
Daiwa	16.4	22.5	15.6	22.1	33.4	49.6

Source: Daiwa Securities & Asian Finance

A Sheltered Childhood

Unlike Japanese banks, which have profited from the Japanese preference for debt financing, Japanese securities firms have not had the benefit of a strong corporate preference for their product as a major source of financing. The attachment to revolving loan financing that so benefited the banks did not support the development of a strong securities industry in Japan. However, there has been an offsetting factor that has helped the Japanese securities industry overcome this fundamental weakness: the protection provided by government regulation.

One of the most direct forms of protection is the fixed commission schedule enjoyed by firms in Japanese securities markets. Although other major financial centres have allowed negotiated commissions for over a decade, Tokyo lags behind with a commission rate structure that in some cases charges more than twice that which could be obtained in other major centres. The effect of this is twofold: the high commissions provide the securities firms with an artificially high level of profitability, and it effectively prevents foreign competitors from using price cutting as a means of taking business away from the Japanese securities firms, which in turn means that foreign securities firms are often doomed to mediocre results given Japanese nationalism and strong traditional business ties.

To further prevent aggressive western securities firms from gaining the upper hand in Japan, limits were placed on the scope of their activities there. It was only in 1986 that foreign firms were first allowed to become members of the TSE and to trade shares directly. Prior to that, foreign firms had to pay 27% of their commissions to Japanese brokers who performed the trades. Even with the relaxation of that rule, a seat on the TSE is by no means a gold mine for foreign brokers. The steep price of the seat (approximately 10 times the cost of a seat on the New York Stock Exchange) and the low volumes generated by foreign brokers render an investment in a seat of dubious value at best. Moreover, even if a seat is finally acquired, there is still little chance of foreign securities firms getting their hands on any of the lucrative postal savings system's money, which is tightly controlled and managed by an inner core of privileged Japanese securities firms. "This is the only important account for us," complains one American investment banker, "and it is being left entirely to the Japanese."(3)

Probably the most important form of protection afforded to securities firms in Japan, however, has been the legal separation of the activities of banks and securities companies. In the wake of the world-wide trend towards equity financing and investing, securities companies have been able to snap up business that twenty years ago would have belonged to the banks, and there is little that the banks can do about it but wait impatiently for the pace of Japanese deregulation to speed up. But Article 65, which enforces the separation of banks and securities houses, is not likely to change soon. The securities companies will resist any relaxation of their monopoly in the Japanese securities industry for as long as possible, knowing quite well that if the separation were lifted, a large chunk of their business would go back to the banks again because the strength of their *keiretsu* group positions. Nomura, in particular, is striving to develop its own captive underwriting clientele that will not shift after the final deregulation is effected, perhaps in five to ten years. In other words, Nomura is actively building its own *keiretsu* of non-industrial companies in a variety of sectors including real estate, insurance, distribution, research, training and advertising.

The Midas Touch

Japanese brokerage firms have used the worldwide trend towards securitization and new, more sophisticated financing techniques to their full advantage. They have seen a huge increase in their basic business of buying and selling shares. A major part of this business has always been the sale of Japanese shares to western investors eager to hitch a ride on the successful Japanese economic locomotive. This business provides Japanese brokers with large, protected profits to be used for expansion elsewhere. It has been estimated that American institutional investments abroad will increase by 400% over the next seven years, with about one-third of it going to Japan.(4) Part of the reason for this foreign interest has been the superior performance of the Tokyo stock market, which has been a remarkably consistent performer over the past two decades. In 1985, for instance, a Japanese-equity mutual fund showed the top mutual fund performance in Canada. Loud pronouncements of such results in financial publications, along with a strong consensus that the yen will continue to appreciate, convince many westerners to put their money into Japanese securities.

Table 6-3

Japanese Investment in Foreign Securities, 1982-1986

(Millions of US$)

Year	Stocks			Bonds		
	Purchase	Sale	Net	Purchase	Sale	Net
1982	1,126	975	151	16,981	10,905	6,076
1983	2,106	10,447	659	22,907	10,400	12,507
1984	1,570	1,518	51	56,347	29,575	26,772
1985	5,483	4,490	993	291,339	237,860	53,479
1986	7,617	4,759	2,858	662,836	618,120	44,716

The above represents figures through licensed securities companies in Japan only.
Source: Wood Gundy

71

The opposite side of the coin is the Japanese purchases of foreign securities, and it is in this area where the securities houses are bound to experience further rapid growth. With a rising supply of Japanese capital needing a home, and the increasing sophistication of Japanese investors, Japanese trades in foreign securities have been growing rapidly as Japanese investors scramble for higher returns than the traditional savings vehicles can offer. As such conditions persist, and as savings are likely to lose their tax-free status under proposed legislation, the volume of activity should swell even further. These Japanese purchases are concentrated in the United States, and traditionally take the form of bonds, although equities are becoming increasingly popular (Table 6-3). This will translate into a real bonanza for Japanese securities companies. In the past three years alone, Japanese purchase of foreign securities through Japanese brokers has risen from $373 million to $917 million.(5) And the Big Four securities houses now account for nearly one-quarter of all underwriting in the buoyant Eurobond market, where borrowers raised some $137 billion in 1985, far more than in the domestic U.S. bond market. As recently as five years ago, it was rare to see a Japanese name among major underwriters of Eurobonds; by the first quarter of 1987, Nomura had leapt to first place among Eurobond lead managers, and the other Japanese giants rank high among the top ten.

Sowing Wild Oats

Although the Japanese securities firms have become large players in the international financial markets, foreign operations still account for only a small proportion of their profits—8% in the case of Nomura. As the profits in Japan (in yen!) continue to reach record highs, the major securities firms will accumulate vast resources to be used to finance international expansion into a position of market leadership. All of the Big Four are concentrating on their international operations as a major source of growth. And it is the prospect of that fixation of Japanese sights on western capital markets that should give Wall Street cause for grave concern.

Nomura Securities sees international expansion as a major corporate commitment, and is making long-term investments in language and cultural training to meet that commitment. In 1985, Nomura Securities Co. demonstrated its dedication to complete internationalization by becoming the second largest recruiter of new graduates at Oxford and Cambridge in England, exceeded only by the British Government.

Although such investments in personnel are enormously expensive and do not provide immediate benefits, they are nevertheless deemed to be worthwhile for Nomura in their pursuit of a totally international capability. On the other side of the Atlantic, the patient, long-term outlook of Japanese securities firms' U.S. branches, many of which have been in place for over a decade with little in the way of profits to show for it, is further evidence of their determination.

Like the Japanese banks, Japanese securities companies are using low margins as a competitive weapon to gain market share. The protected domestic Japanese market with its rich commission schedule and steadily increasing volume is providing the muscle that allows their foreign operations to drive into new markets with cut-throat prices. "They've simply gone out and bought market share, using their massive profits in the Tokyo market to subsidize loss-making Eurobond deals," said one competitor recently.(6)

An enormous asset of the Japanese securities companies in their international expansion is their placement power back in Japan. The ability of the Japanese securities companies to take large parcels of new share issues and distribute them quickly to an investments-hungry population has enabled them to entice foreign firms to place new issues with them. Without such a placement base in Japan, foreign securities firms cannot hope to get their hands on significant amounts of the surplus Japanese capital. The Japanese securities firms are able to unload large parcels of shares through their employment of Japanese women as salespeople to approach and build up strong relationships with "Mrs. Watanabe," the proverbial Japanese housewife, who has shown herself to be a keen and shrewd investor. During the past two years, Nomura has placed substantial pieces of IBM, Saipem, Jaguar, and Norsk Data, among others, in this way. Similarly, Yamaichi has completed placements for Coca-Cola and Nestle.(7)

The Japanese securities firms are also sparing no efforts to expand their activities abroad, exploiting every opportunity that the relatively open U.S. and European markets afford them. Three of the top four Japanese securities firms have had seats on the New York Stock Exchange for several years now, and requests by Nomura and Daiwa for primary dealer status with the U.S. Federal Reserve Board have recently been granted. The granting of such a status requires a member to maintain large daily transaction volumes (over $300 million) through the whole spectrum of government bonds on the market, and requires a large investment in computerized trading equipment and personnel to operate it. Receiving primary dealership status will allow the Japanese firms access to U.S. Treasury bonds at lower prices than if they had to buy through an intermediary, as well as information and recognition. The information is acquired in meetings with Federal officials and traders, who discuss their impressions and policies in the markets, and also through the use of special trading screens reserved for the exclusive use of primary dealers.(8) The ability of the Japanese to meet these requirements in a foreign market is an indication of their new-found international financial presence.

Not content with just the healthy gains derived from their traditional business areas, the Japanese securities firms are also aggressively pursuing other types of lucrative opportunities abroad which are denied them at home. One such example is the case of Daiwa Securities Co., which started up a trust bank, Daiwa Trust, in New Jersey in early 1986. Nomura Securities Co. staged a major coup at the same time by getting a commercial banking license in London after a shrewd tit-for-tat deal with the British Government. Japan's Ministry of Finance appears to turn a blind or at least a lenient eye towards such bending of Japan's domestic rules dividing banking and securities business, as long as it happens overseas. By taking advantage of such opportunities, Japanese securities companies can gain valuable experience, studying foreign methods and adapting and perfecting them for their own use. Then, using price as a competitive weapon, they can proceed to claim large segments of the market.

Conclusion

Although the influence of Japanese securities firms will certainly grow, there is still some doubt as to what extent they can duplicate the innovative qualities of competitive western firms that have already gone through a period of deregulation in their home markets, rendering them more creative and flexible in response to the increased competition. The Japanese consensus system of decision-making, their emphasis on memorization and attention to detail over creativity and independent thinking, and their lack of rewards for individual performance have led some foreign competitors to feel that the Japanese lack the agility and individual initiative required to succeed in the dynamic securities business.

Hiring non-Japanese wheelers and dealers away from the leading American and European financial houses has been of only limited success for the Japanese in overcoming these handicaps. The culture shock—for both parties involved—leads to very high turnover, and even the high salary premiums which the Japanese pay have not been sufficiently attractive to hold specialists. One response of the Japanese to this perceived weakness is to try to help top western universities produce graduates more in tune with Japanese culture and business methods. In 1986, for example, Nomura Securities Co. endowed both a $1.6 million chair to Massachusetts Institute of Technology and a $1.5 million chair to New York University. While such support of higher education is laudable, one may assume that the Japanese donors expect to recoup their investments at some time in the future by gaining access to graduates more attentive to Japanese ways and needs (an assumption entirely consistent with the very long-term profit horizons of most large Japanese firms).

Although deregulation and increased exposure to foreign techniques should help the securities firms to compensate for what may be weaknesses in some areas, many foreigners believe that "if deregulation pits Americans against Japanese on a level playing field, U.S. financial institutions can hold the line—if not gain ground."(9) But will that "level playing field" ever materialize? New York and London have both undergone waves of deregulation which benefit the Japanese among others. But in Japan—even with the banks feeling the pinch of saturated domestic markets and progressive deregulation—the Big Four securities houses will resist for years to come any erosion of their profitable base; and the cash they will keep on generating over the next few years will give them in any event a major advantage. By the time really effective deregulation does come about, we may have learned that what we took as liberalization of the Japanese financial market was little more than a cleverly-designed lure, as the next chapter explains.

1. Gary Hector, "The Japanese Want to Be Your Banker," *Fortune*, October 27, 1986, p. 97.
2. "The Brokers," *Echo de la Bourse*, April 23, 1987.
3. David Lake, "Japanese Brokers Secure a Firm Foothold in U.S. Market," *Asian Finance*, March 15, 1986, p. 34.
4. "Now Japan Wants to Conquer Global Finance." *Business Week*, April 8, 1985, p. 58.
5. Ibid., p. 33.
6. "Nomura Dominates Eurobond Market," *Financial Times*, April 14, 1987.

7. "Now, the Japanese Attack the World's Financial Markets," *Euromoney,* October 1985, p. 79.

8. Terry Dodsworth, "Nikko Seeks Primary Dealer Status," *Financial Times,* December 6, 1985.

9. "Now Japan Wants to Conquer Global Finance," op. cit., p. 59.

CHAPTER 7

Deregulation: Japan Inc.'s Trojan Horse

Beware the Japanese bearing gifts! Liberalization of Japan's financial markets is often wrapped in the guise of concessions to foreigners, but it is shrewdly crafted to derive maximum benefits for the Japanese themselves.

a toast to the opening of the financial markets in japan.

There is no doubt that Japan has a much more liberalized financial services market today than it had ten years ago. And there is also no doubt that the trend towards liberalization of Japanese financial markets will continue into the future, as Japan's international economy demands increasingly internationalized financial markets. What is not so well known is the impact of that decontrol, and how the whole process is guided by Japan's Ministry of Finance (MoF). The evidence strongly indicates that the Japanese readily deregulate if it is to their advantage, but drag their heels indefinitely on liberalization if it affects weak sectors which could face severe difficulties if suddenly confronted by tougher foreign (or even domestic) competition. The very terms employed by the Japanese indicate their reluctance to let go the reins too much too quickly. To them, the term is "liberalization" of financial services markets, implying a certain amount of generosity on their part in allowing what changes there are to have occurred at all; whereas to westerners, the phrase usually heard is "deregulation," with connotations of legal fairness and reciprocity.

The primary purpose of protectionist regulation in Japan has always been safety: safety from bankruptcy for the financial institutions involved in the various segregated financial sectors, and safety of depositors' and investors' funds. Safety, however, is the antithesis of high rates of return and efficiency, and high rates of return and efficiency are what Japan increasingly needs. It used to be that the most efficient and high-yielding investment for Japanese capital was in the factories and infrastructure required to create the economic powerhouse that Japan has become. Segregating financial institutions and limiting competition for deposits kept the cost of funds to industry artificially low, promoting growth. But that is no longer the case.

The rules of the game have changed because the best opportunities now lie elsewhere. The world is now a financial supermarket through which the Japanese can roam at will, selecting the choicest cuts and the daintiest morsels. But the Japanese financial system is only designed to supply a few locally-produced products to the domestic market, a rather bland collection of products that are not in step with the requirements of a sophisticated population beginning to enjoy the fruits of their labor. It is this dilemma of feeding a financial products-hungry population while still protecting a myriad of small and large Japanese financial producers who can't protect themselves from each other or from the foreign institutions howling out in the cold, that is so difficult for the MoF to adjust to. To date, it appears as though the MoF has decided to entice the foreigners in by throwing a few morsels their way, and then, while the foreigners are relishing their scanty meal, slowly draining them of their talents and skills. And it is quite likely that by the time the doors are thrown wide open, the rejuvenated domestic Japanese industry will be quite strong and ferocious enough to fend off any sort of attack which the foreigners might mount—and maybe even do a little marauding of its own.

MoF at the Helm

There are some very logical reasons why this tense state of affairs exists today. The Japanese financial system was modelled after the American system of separation of the four financial pillars of commercial banking, investment banking, insurance, and trust banking. But whereas the American and European financial systems were forced to open up and deregulate to varying degrees in the 1970s and 80s in response to growing economic strength and international activities, the Japanese, starting from scratch with a war-ravaged economy at the end of World War II, did not really require a world-class financial system until recently. Furthermore, typical Japanese conservatism and resistance to change by the "old guard" management who had experienced the lean years after the war helped to suppress any pressures for change. Thus, while their American and European counterparts were undergoing trial by the refiner's fire of free competition, Japan's financial institutions, with their separated markets and government protection, were left largely untouched. Therefore, if the Japanese had allowed deregulation to move too quickly, there might well have been dire consequences for Japanese financial institutions suddenly confronted with the lean, mean, and innovative survivors of western deregulation. The Japanese authorities evidently decided that it was better to sacrifice the principles of free markets and "survival of the fittest" than to lose their financial markets to foreigners.

That thinking persists today. A prime example is the Japanese reluctance to completely liberalize the rate of interest allowed on deposits. Although some movement has been made in this direction with the freeing of interest rates on large deposits (currently those over 300 million yen or $2 million), ordinary deposits still earn surprisingly meager rates of return.(1) Abrupt deregulation of interest rates could be particularly painful, if not lethal, for many of the smaller city and regional banks. Complete interest rate liberalization would mean competitive bidding for depositors' funds. Interest rates that these smaller banks would have to pay to depositors would have nowhere to go but up from their current artificially low levels. With their costs of funds rising and no corresponding increase in profitable lending opportunities, the possibility of collapse for such banks would become all too real. As ruler of a banking system that has not experienced a bank failure since World War II, the MoF would not find such a scenario very easy to swallow.(2) Since foreign banks are effectively prevented from tapping into this low-cost source of funds through MoF restrictions, they can make little headway against their Japanese counterparts. By allowing deposit rates to rise only gradually, the MoF is preventing large-scale failures of Japanese banks unable to earn large enough margins as their funding costs rise.

"Come Into My Web," Said the Spider to the Fly

In some cases, the Japanese financial institutions are not in such weak positions, and can easily withstand foreign competition. In such cases, the entry of foreign competitors can actually help the Japanese by providing them with new skills and honing their competitive instincts. The Japanese government has been truly masterful at enticing selected foreign financial institutions to the dazzling potential of the Tokyo financial markets, while constraining their freedom sufficiently for them to have no real possibility of taking away significant business from their Japanese competitors.

The most vivid example of this was the opening up of the Japanese trust banking (pension fund management) business to foreigners in 1985. Foreign trust banks—generally considered more highly skilled and progressive than their Japanese counterparts—had for years been clamoring for access to managing the massive Japanese pension fund portfolios. With Japan's rapidly-ageing population and inadequate public pension programmes, private savings earmarked for pension funds are experiencing explosive growth. One estimate is that pension fund assets could reach 20 trillion yen ($140 billion) by 1988, and 50 trillion yen (almost $360 billion) by 2010. As mentioned earlier (Chapter 5), the Japanese government eventually agreed, with an appropriate show of reluctance, to allow nine foreign trust banks to operate in Japan. But the deck was stacked against them from the start. By requiring the foreign firms "to employ staff knowledgeable of Japanese trust business, particularly pension fund business," the government virtually forced the foreign firms into joint ventures with Japanese trust banks. The foreign entrants stood little chance of making any substantial profits because of the long-term nature of the pension-fund management business, the strong ties between fund managers and clients, and Japanese pension funds' historic emphasis on security (as opposed to high yields, which is what the foreigners essentially had to offer). The average fee charged by Japanese fund-managing banks is about 0.8%. In order for the foreign entrants to take business away from the Japanese competition, they would, in the opinion of one foreign observer, have to undercut the Japanese with fees as low as 0.1%.(3) At that fee level, however, the foreigners would have to generate many times the volume of the Japanese fund-managing banks just to be profitable. The main result of all of this has been a substantial flow of skills and expertise to the Japanese trust banks, while their reluctant foreign partners have little but hope that the situation will change in the future. As one Tokyo-based foreign-banking consultant bluntly put it: "The Japanese are going to suck the foreigners dry and then spit them out."(4)

The determination of the Japanese government to continue denying full access to foreign financial institutions was illustrated dramatically as recently as March 1987, when the Japanese Ministry of Health and Welfare (MHW) announced it would continue to exclude foreign trust banks from management of its pension funds. The Ministry said that the foreign trust banks "had not yet accumulated enough experience in Japan to be entrusted with pension funds."(5) The ruling has provoked angry but so far ineffective responses from the nine foreign trust banks. Robert Binney, senior vice-president of Chase Manhattan, called on the Ministry to consider the banks' worldwide experience: "Clearly our experience in Japan is not that long, but we have been in the trust banking business for forty years and feel we can bring an expertise that Japanese trust banks do not have."(6) Robert Sharp, president of Manufacturers Hanover Trust Bank, agrees, claiming that the foreign trust banks are bringing much more to Japan in terms of good pension fund practice than they are taking out.

The Heat is On

Of course, not everyone is content with this rather lop-sided state of affairs, and the MoF is finding itself under attack from all sides to make the rules of the game more fair. One source of pressure is the foreign institutions who want access to a greater scope of activities in Japan, although it is usually only when these firms' cries are taken up by their respective governments (along with the threat of reciprocal protectionist legislation in their home markets) that the MoF really pays them any heed. Sometimes the pressure takes the form of applications for licenses that the MoF might regard as on or across the borderline of acceptable segregation of financial institutions. Some foreign firms are aware that the MoF does not want to be seen as constantly turning down foreign applications in the eyes of the rest of the world. In 1983, Citibank scored a major success when it was able to sneak by Japanese regulations preventing banks from engaging in securities business by buying Vickers da Costa, a British securities firm in Japan. The deal was announced during President Reagan's visit to Japan so that a Japanese veto of the deal would be very embarrassing on a political level.(7)

However, it has proven to be very difficult for foreign governments to force any significant change of heart upon the MoF, at least in the short run, because of the complexity of trade in financial services, Japanese stonewalling, and major differences in opinion as to what reciprocity actually means. The Americans claim—correctly—that Citicorp and Merrill Lynch are not permitted to do in Tokyo what Dai-Ichi Kangyo and Nomura can do in New York. The Japanese politely respond that they treat a Merrill Lynch in Japan exactly as they treat a Nomura: according to the Japanese book of rules. The settlement of such conflicts almost always entails countless studies and long negotiations, not to mention an enormous amount of political posturing and pandering to special interest groups. Before the Japanese treat Dai-Ichi Kangyo and Citicorp the same way as both are treated in New York or London, many years of cherry blossoms will have brightened the wonderful spring season in Japan!

In another case, the British were able to turn the tables on the Japanese and use the same stonewalling technique to their own advantage. The British were angered by what they saw as an unfair restriction of their firms' activities in Tokyo. There, British firms were restricted to either banking or securities businesses, whereas Japanese firms want to be able to engage in both the banking and securities business in London. The British authorities responded by holding up the granting of banking licenses to Japanese securities firms eager to take advantage of London's free and easy regulations. It is in such cases where direct retaliation is at issue that the Japanese are most likely to sit up and take notice.

However, the most persuasive force for change in the Japanese financial system will probably come from the Japanese themselves. First, there are the Japanese corporations who already dominate their particular field, and who could benefit by increased freedom to engage in new sorts of activities in Japan. Japanese banks and securities companies would both dearly love to sink their teeth into each others' markets. The large commercial banks are particularly impatient to move into new areas after having witnessed the steady erosion of their client base through the efforts of the securities firms and the world-wide trend towards securitization. They accurately believe that the future belongs to those who can meet all of a client's particular needs, be it loans, bonds (and swaps), or equity issues. Furthermore, the many different divisions between city banks, trust banks, regional banks, sogo banks and others is creating all sorts of friction among banks clamouring for access to each others' turf, and those under attack are just as adamant in demanding continued protection. Both banks and securities companies are eyeing the Japanese pension fund management industry as an area of particular interest—an area where they could probably claim a significant market share by using the many resources available to them.

A second source of pressure from within Japan is the Japanese consumer of financial services, who, increasingly frustrated by low rates of return, lack of flexibility, and the very limited variety of financial instruments available, will demand a first-class financial system to match a first-class economy. These pressures will set the stage for a conflict between a myriad of interests in and out of Japan for the years to come.

Limiting the Damage

Even when the Japanese do make concessions, they have some favorite tactics to limit the damage, or even to further their own interests. One such tactic is stonewalling. In much the same way as corporations stretch their accounts payable, the Japanese stretch out the timetable of change by subdividing major concessions into small manageable parts, making changes on an individual case basis, and by simply taking time to "study" the matter further. Such foot-dragging has been proven to have a very real economic payoff for the Japanese. A major study completed in early 1985 used a sophisticated computer model that combined political and economic variables to assess the effect of liberalization. The study concluded:

> Foot-dragging over liberalization has a real economic payoff for the Japanese. Real growth rates for the 1985-87 period are forecast to be a full 1.2 percent higher than if Japan liberalized. This is a cumulative US$50 billion plus in GNP for the same period.(8)

Time *is* money for the Japanese!

Another favorite tactic is to make a small concession in an area where they will not really be adversely affected, and where they might well benefit (as in the trust banking industry), and dress it up as a major victory for the foreigners. Then, this can be used as leverage to force western markets to open further to Japanese interests. Meanwhile, the areas of the Japanese market where western firms could really score big are protected as usual.

Still another source of foreign frustration is the value of the yen. By preventing the yen from becoming a truly internationalized currency, some foreigners argue, the Japanese are able to maintain the yen at an artificially low level. Extensive trade and investments in non-yen currencies increase the demand for those currencies and push up their value, rendering Japanese exports less expensive than their non-yen counterparts. This in turn contributes to Japanese trade surpluses, which in turn cause massive capital exports, which keeps the yen low and so on. An American Senator has commented, "There is deep concern in Congress over our trade deficit. We are truly seeing a deindustrialization of America—are we just to be hotel managers or run Burger King stands? Does the answer lie in Japan's capital markets?"(9)

Similar logic can be applied to Japanese interest rates. With interest rates held at artificially low levels, capital is attracted away from Japan to other high-yielding centers. And again this contributes to a low yen and higher levels of exports.

Interestingly enough, the Japanese lose in this process just as the foreigners do. By maintaining these inefficient barriers between financial institutions and propping up noncompetitive firms, the Japanese are depriving themselves of the best in financial services which they deserve. Low returns on bank deposits and pension funds, poor customer service, and artificially low-priced exports represent in effect an economic redirection of capital from individuals, who could use it to purchase more goods and services and to improve their standard of living, to banks and other financial institutions who use the funds to make loans to and buy securities from foreigners, improving *their* standard of living in the process. In essence, the Japanese are exporting their standard of living to the West, while the West experiences unemployment with its attendant hardships. How western firms can help the Japanese see the error of their ways, while protecting their business from further erosion by the Japanese in the bargain, is the subject of the concluding chapters.

1. *Japan Economic Journal*, September 13, 1986, p. D35.
2. Richard Hanson, "Think the Unthinkable," *Far Eastern Economc Review*, June 27, 1985, pp. 90-91.
3. Bruce Roscoe, "Foreigners Think Twice About the Latest Liberalism," *Far Eastern Economic Review*, April 25, 1985, pp. 61-62.
4. David Lascelles, "The Rise and Rise of the Cut-Price Lenders," *Financial Times*, February 12, 1986, p. 2.
5. "Japan Curbs Foreign Trust Banks," *Financial Times*, March 20, 1987.
6. Ibid.
7. "Citibank In Japan: A-Wooing", *The Economist*, March 1, 1986, p. 72.
8. Dennis Holden, "Foot-Dragging in Japan's Capital Markets," *Asiabanking*, October 1985, p. 70.
9. Ibid.

CHAPTER 8

The Termite Strategy

The Japanese financial services sector is embarking on a strategy directly comparable to that which placed the Land of the Rising Sun in the forefront of the information technology market. Their approach can be summarized succinctly as *the Termite Strategy*.

The Termite Strategy invokes no master plan, and no single leader to orchestrate the steps. And yet, just as termites are blind but still able to work diligently towards a common goal, the Japanese financial services houses are all driving towards the same target, each seeking to maximize its strengths and minimize its weaknesses to the greatest possible degree, searching out the areas of greatest demand and paths of least resistance from competitors. Under the Termite Strategy there is no big thrust for the target, no single front line, but thousands of small steps. Regardless of the counterstrategy used by the competition, the advance seems to move inexorably on.

The purpose of this chapter is to summarize the steps the Japanese are and will be taking to dominate the market for financial services, through

a comparison with their successful strategy in the information technology market. The analogy is astoundingly clear.

The Termite Strategy may be summarized as follows:

(1) Japanese identify segments of industry, and choose an appropriate entry segment.

(2) They join with foreign competition in other segments of the industry where foreign know-how or technology is superior to that of the Japanese. These joint-ventures enable the Japanese to gain important expertise in their own market before competing head-on in foreign markets.

(3) They build up a strong distribution infrastructure.

(4) After establishing themselves in foreign markets through high quality and low prices, they are accused of "dumping." They engineer political deals and, at the request of foreign governments, they raise prices. Increased prices mean higher profits to Japan, as well as to foreign competition, at the expense of the consumer.

(5) Surplus profits from increased prices provide the capital for the Japanese to manufacture or operate abroad rather than exporting Japanese products or services. The Japanese ensure that high-value-added operations remain at home in Japan, with mainly assembly-type operations abroad. Profits and expertise flow back to Japan, while lower-value-added jobs formerly lost to Japanese competition are reinstated abroad under the umbrella of Japanese investments.

(6) Finally, the Japanese engage in take-overs to rescue failing companies, and finance research and scholarships at leading western universities to secure access to brilliant, well-trained young graduates, educated to meet Japanese requirements.

The two tables which follow compare the Termite Strategy used so successfully in information technology to the approach being taken in the financial services industry today. They succinctly summarize all the key elements and stages of the Termite Strategy explained in this chapter. We encourage the reader to refer frequently to the tables while reading the chapter.

Table 8-1

ELEMENTS OF COMPETITIVE ANALYSIS

What is the nature of the segment most attractive to the Japanese?

1. a segment where the financial resources of the competition will not permit major resistance and counter attack to the Japanese assault on that segment.
2. a segment characterized by double-digit growth (i.e. enormous volume).
3. a highly price-sensitive segment
4. a segment where entry risk for Japanese is low, and with few barriers to entry
5. a segment which provides an entry ticket to other segments.

What are the segments of the information technology and financial services market?

INFORMATION TECHNOLOGY	FINANCIAL SERVICES
1. Semi-conductors (chips)	1. Government lending

2. personal computers
    peripherals
    minicomputers
    mainframe computers
    communications equipment
	2. foreign exchange
	    underwriting
	    stock exchange operations
	    trust banking

3. software	3. mergers and acquisitions

What are the 5 characteristics of the semiconductor and government lending markets?

SEMICONDUCTORS	GOVERNMENT LENDING
1. small number of competitors	1. few lenders have enough cash to supply demand
2. standardized high-unit volume	2. huge government appetite requiring a similar approach
3. price sensitive	3. price sensitive
4. low risk, if only surplus products are sold to outsiders	4. low risk as governments generally do not go bankrupt
5. major entry ticket to other information technology products	5. important for the creation of political goodwill

What are the 2 key factors for success in semiconductors and government lending?

SEMICONDUCTORS	GOVERNMENT LENDING
1. product reliability	1. placement capacity
2. low price	2. low margins over LIBOR

Table 8-2

The Termite Strategy

Information Technology

1. Japanese enter the Information Technology market through high volume price-sensitive semiconductor segment where competition has least resistance due to their focus on financial returns instead of market share.

2. Japanese move into supplier contracts and OEM agreements penetrating other segments of the Information Technology market such as personal computers, peripherals, office equipment... to acquire manufacturing expertise.

3. Japanese first secure their market through independent distributors, then establish direct sales channels centrally controlled by the Japanese headquarters.

4. After acquiring a major market share the Japanese are accused of "dumping". They engineer political agreements which safeguard their market position and raise their profitability while Western competitors feel that the "steamroller" has been stopped. The Japanese market will be "opened" for sophisticated chips the Japanese do not YET manufacture.

5. Japanese establish joint ventures and invest in new assembly lines, making sure that high-value added operations remain in Japan, while overseas profits increase in relative importance. They also build the largest research and development institutes in the world.

6. Japanese consolidate their leadership-position by rescuing bankrupt manufacturers, often at the demand of Western governments, and even engage in hostile take-overs. They heavily finance fundamental research in artificial intelligence at leading Western universities and channel the results back to Japan.

Financial services

1. Japanese enter the Financial Services market through government lending segment where margins are crucial and the governments' appetite seems insatiable. Huge balance of trade and savings are channelled to foreign governments creating political goodwill.

2. Japanese join with financial houses in other segments of the Financial Services market such as foreign exchange, trust and retail banking, leasing... to acquire financial engineering expertise.

3. Japanese build up large infrastructure through representative offices and branches. Offices are managed by Japanese staff under Tokyo's direct supervision.

4. After acquiring a leading market share, Japanese WILL BE accused of "dumping". They engineer political deals which will "open" the Japanese financial markets. But these will be either saturated (e.g. banking) or where foreign expertise is most needed.

5. Japanese financial houses obtain banking licences, primary dealer status, seats on the NYSE & LSE, and dominate the minor financial centres, all through bilateral deals. Profit and expertise flow back to Japan. They build their own think tanks.

6. Japanese consolidate their market share by rescuing bankrupt financial houses and even make hostile take-over bids. They offer millions of dollars through university endowments to secure long term access to well-trained bright graduates, more tailored to their needs.

INFORMATION TECHNOLOGY

Reconnaissance

An appropriate entry segment, according to the Japanese, would be a segment where the financial resources of the competition are insufficient to block the Japanese penetration of that segment. The Japanese seek a segment with high growth potential, as high volume is necessary to their success due to the huge volume capacity at their disposal through the captive, protected home markets provided by their *keiretsu* groups. As they use price to capture a large market share quickly, it is important that the segment be highly price-sensitive. They optimally want an area where there are few barriers to entry, and where the entry risk *to the Japanese* is low. Finally, they seek a prime target segment which will open doors to the rest of the industry. These criteria are summarised in the first section of Table 8-1.

A simplified outline of the information technology market could identify seven sub-sectors (see Table 8-1, second section): semiconductors (chips), personal computers, minicomputers, mainframe computers, peripherals (i.e. printers, cables etc.), communications equipment, and software.

For their initial approach to the market, the Japanese were not interested in the software market, where they had performed poorly in the past and were definitely not in a position to undercut the leadership of cash-rich European and American competitors who were setting world standards, such as Lotus, Microsoft, Logica, and Cap Gemini Sogeti. This segment has not yet been tackled. The mainframe market, which even in Japan was dominated until recently by Big Blue IBM, did not appeal to them either as an entry segment, nor did the personal computer (PC) market led by Apple and IBM. These segments became the secondary targets. No, the Japanese carefully selected the semiconductor market as their first target in the information technology industry. Why? The American competition was leading, but they were stand-alone companies, not integrated into large conglomerates as the Japanese are in their *keiretsu* groups, with their large captive markets. The Americans had to pursue a competitive strategy predicated on short-term profitability, to satisfy the cash-flow and dividend targets set by private investors and venture-capitalists. The Japanese could aim simply for *volume;* they had their captive markets within the *keiretsu,* and whatever sales they made outside their group could be priced on the basis of marginal cost. Moreover, the basic semiconductor segment provided an ideal springboard to other, more sophisticated sectors of information technology. (The reader should, from this point, follow the sequence of Table 8-2.)

The First Assault

Following this initial game plan, the Japanese chipmakers were able to successfully undercut the market. As expected, the economies of scale reached by the extra sales abroad served to accelerate their learning curve in production and applications. For example, Matsushita uses 80-90% of the semiconductors it produces; the remaining 10-20% sold overseas allows them to recoup extra research and development costs, pays for the marketing of the chips, and—perhaps most important—helps Matsushita to get a feel for the information technology market on an international basis. Unlike their American competitors, they did not have to worry about the huge capital investments needed to shift from the 8 to the 16 to the 32 and 64 bit chips; there is always cash available within the group to expand production into areas of high demand. The consumer sought low price and high product reliability, and the Japanese provided exactly that. They supplied a quality product in high unit volume at a low price. And the market kept on growing while a small number of competitors fought to maintain their share.

Branching Out

At the same time as the Japanese semiconductor manufacturers built up their market share in chips, forced prices down, and proved to clients that their product reliability was the best and their price the lowest, they were able to develop a parallel strategy of supplier contracts with original equipment manufacturers (OEMs) in other market segments, thus gaining valuable manufacturing expertise in related sectors (Table 8-2, Step 2). Slowly but steadily the Japanese took control not just of the semiconductor market, but of other segments of the information technology market as well, such as microcomputers, peripherals, and mainframes.

Parallel to this, the Japanese improved their distribution system (Table 8-2, Step 3). The initial presence of the Japanese through independent distributors gave way to wholly-owned subsidiaries for distribution and after-sales service. They then proceeded to consolidate their market position by replacing American computers with Japanese models in government agencies at home and in some selected countries. Hitachi, for example, offered 50-60% discounts in Japan (of course), Brazil, Spain and Australia. They knew that once they had obtained a major market share of the government sector in those countries, the private sector would follow, purchasing their computers at higher prices. After all, one has to be concerned about dumping charges while selling to the private sector, whereas governments will never object to receiving computers for less than cost. Would any government ever consider filing a dumping charge against cheap access to information technology?

The Politics of Price

Soon after, in the wake of increasing pressure from Japanese competition and the apparent need for western companies to enter into coalitions with the Japanese, the cry arose from European and North American manufacturers: "The Japanese are dumping semiconductors." The Japanese invasion of the memory chip market between 1973 and 1975 and later on between 1981 and 1983 in the 64k memory market triggered appeals for help, as the Japanese just seemed to be able to produce at a lower cost. On the basis of battles lost in the past, western companies began to delegate production of their chips to the Japanese at the start of new projects, rather than fight a costly price war after large investments had been made in new production facilities.

Governments were pushed to block the Japanese out of the chip market and to levy an extra tax on their products. In order to avoid the embarrassment of a dumping charge, the Japanese diligently shifted into their "political engineering" gear (Table 8-2, Step 4), working out an agreement on price and volume with the American private and public sectors. In the fall of 1985 the Reagan administration "persuaded" Japan to sign a five-year agreement to stop dumping chips below "cost" (according to American accounting standards) and to make its own semiconductor market more open to foreign manufacturers. But the pact generated sharp controversy from the outset over its side effects, and American charges of Japanese non-compliance led to the imposition of special retaliatory tariffs in the spring of 1987.

The outcome of the agreement was, of course, increased cost to the American consumer and increased profits for Japan. The chip-deal between the U.S. and Japan resulted in an immediate average price rise of some 20% for semiconductors, with some chips even tripling in sales price. By forcing chip prices in the market dramatically upward, the pact could severely harm the competitive ability of other high-tech industries in the U.S.A. whose products contain semiconductors. And since the Japanese are no longer allowed to offer cut-throat prices on chips, they can increase their profit margins handsomely, thanks to the largesse of western policy makers!

This additional profit from the consumer permits the Japanese to invest in chip factories in the U.S. (Table 8-2, Step 5), in much the same way that they began investing in automobile plants in the U.S. after similar experiences in the automobile industry. There, the Japanese were asked to go for a voluntary auto-restraint agreement on their exports, which allowed them—through the game of supply and demand—to increase their sales tag by some $1000 per car. After three years this extra income generated from the American consumer permitted the Japanese to begin building assembly plants in the U.S. But the higher-value-added elements of car design and manufacture remain in Japan, as do the project-engineering and the production-process skills that underlie competitive success—the result of an implicit strategy of keeping the higher-paying, higher-value-added jobs in Japan. And for the sake of creating employment at whatever cost, the U.S. and Europe are happy to be delegated the lower-value-added assembly functions. Nissan Motor's $575 million assembly plant in Smyrna, Tennessee, offers a case in point. Although the assembly itself takes place in the U.S., the gear boxes and engine blocks—among the main value-added components—are still sourced from Japan. According to the Japan Economics Institute, by the end of 1986 there were nearly 600 factories in the U.S. in which the Japanese owned a majority stake.

Aftermath

Today, the Japanese export more chips than do American manufacturers, even though the Americans held over half the world market until 1981. As recently as 1982 the American share of the global market for micro chips stood at 49% compared with Japan's 27%. By the end of 1986, Japan had taken the lead with 38% of chip sales versus 35% for the U.S., according to In-Stat, an Arizona-based research firm. U.S. chipmakers do not expect much relief from competition through the agreement to limit dumping chips. They have already turned their attention to types of semiconductors that foreign rivals will find more difficult to copy. The U.S. chipmakers now believe that their future lies in fabricating relatively small batches—thousands instead of millions—of customized chips for specialized uses. Companies like National Semiconductor and Intel are moving away from commodity-like memory chips, to concentrate on microprocessors and other products that perform advanced functions. But at least one company, Texas Instruments, has stubbornly refused to give up the race with the Japanese to make even more densely packed memory chips.

By expanding into products which use a lot of their semiconductors, the Japanese have taken over world leadership of a wide variety of information technology products ranging from photocopiers, typewriters, and other peripheral equipment, to minicomputers; they now challenge even telecommunications and mainframes (which will further enhance their software capabilities, as one-third of the mainframe market is systems software). But, we were warned of this as early as December, 1981 by a Canon executive in a Business Week interview: "We want to offer ALL products." If we had taken them seriously at that time, we could have prepared ourselves better to meet the Japanese challenge in the information technology market.

FINANCIAL SERVICES

The Japanese are now applying the Termite Strategy to the financial services sector. Although we cannot identify the precise steps that they will take, the evidence is there. There is no master plan, but in the end it becomes a clear and well-balanced strategy to get to and stay at the top of the list of the world leaders of financial services. How will they do it?

Let us simplify the financial services sector into some seven categories (Table 8-1): government lending, foreign exchange, investment credits, underwriting, stock exchange operations, trust banking and mergers and acquisitions.

The Japanese will not tackle the financial services market through the mergers and acquisitions segment—this will be the last segment for them to attempt—nor through trust banking, for the Japanese are noted for their inexperience in these sectors, both at home and abroad. Recognizing their limited knowhow, they seek cooperative efforts in those areas, with the full support of their government.

Feeding Uncle Sam

Japan's initial entry into the market for financial services has been mainly through government lending. (Refer again to Table 8-2.) The enormous appetite of governments for extra cash, their somewhat standardized approach to loan deals, and the high volume and high price sensitivity of government lending, all provided the Japanese with enough justification to conclude that this was the place to start. Few competitors can satiate the voracious appetite of governments. In this highly price-sensitive market, the Japanese offered loans priced often only *1/16 of one percent* over their cost of funds, quickly making them the favorite of governments the world over. The county of Los Angeles went to the

Japanese for a $250 million loan, as did the New York Job Development Agency for a $190 million loan arranged by Sumitomo. Furthermore, this favorable government lending gives the Japanese valuable political leverage that comes in handy when a Japanese financial house needs a foreign licence or permit. The Japanese always offer slightly better rates than any other banks, go for minuscule margins, and provide consumer satisfaction in somewhat the same way as they satisfied the man on the street who bought his first Toyota at a discount price and got hooked on a quality product with a long-term warranty.

Goal: The International Financial Supermarket

With government lending well established for Japanese institutions, they have begun to join with foreign financial institutions in other segments of the financial services market such as foreign exchange, stock exchange operations, and trust banking. They are actively acquiring expertise in much the same way that the information technology industry got a feel for the market through the original-equipment-manufacturing agreements. And behind the scenes, the Japanese government helps smooth the way wherever possible.

For example, when trust banking was deregulated in Japan, the Japanese government required that foreign entrants have expertise in Japanese trust banking (see Chapter 7). How could any foreign financial institution have such expertise when the market had always been closed to them? With the traditional life-time employment system and company loyalty in Japan, it was almost impossible for foreign banks to hire away local experts. The only way to meet the requirement was to join forces with a Japanese trust bank: the foreigners offered their sophisticated know-how in return for a ticket to get into the theater. Citibank teamed up with Yasuda Trust and Banking; Chase Manhattan and Manufacturers Hanover with Daiwa Bank; J. Henry Schroeder Bank and Trust was bought up by the Industrial Bank of Japan. The likely results were summed up succinctly by an American banker in Tokyo: "None of the foreign trust banks here are ever going to make much money, but the Japanese are going to learn everything there is to know about trust banking through the joint ventures."

At the same time the Japanese financial institutions began building an impressive international infrastructure. In 1975 the Japanese banks had only 225 branches abroad, but by 1985 this had risen to 716. And those branches are well connected with their headquarters to secure an efficient management of the operations worldwide. Sanwa, just to mention one, invested some $8.4 million over the past two years in SOBAS (Sanwa

Overseas Banking Automation System). The computer and communication technology which the Japanese had available within their *keiretsu* came in handy to set up the needed services infrastructure.

Japanese financial institutions have also embarked on a dramatic series of acquisitions abroad to acquire new expertise and to gain market share. Their aggressive acquisition strategy has so far been limited in Europe to one particular case: the purchase of 52% of Banca Gottardo of Switzerland by the most profitable of the Japanese banks, Sumitomo. Other similar acquisitions are bound to occur as the opportunities arise, particularly following the inevitable shake-out which will result from the Big Bang in London.

Some examples of Japanese acquisitions in the United States are worthwhile enumerating because they give insight into the bold strategy of the Japanese—steps individually conceived and executed, though they all seem to form part of a major coordinated assault on the market:

1983: $475 million purchase of the Chicago-based commercial financing company Walter E. Heller by Fuji Bank.

1985: $520 million purchase of the Continental Illinois leasing subsidiary by Sanwa Bank.

1986: $500 million purchase of 12·5% of Goldman Sachs stock by Sumitomo Bank.

1986: $250 million purchase of the Bank of California by Mitsubishi Bank, which had previously acquired the BanCal Tristate for $282 million.

1986: Bank of Tokyo purchase of California First Bank.

1987: Nippon Life Insurance, the largest life assurance company in Japan, bought a 13% stake in Shearson Lehman Brothers, the securities operation of American Express, for $538 million.

The assault has been well targeted. Today, *half* of the twelve largest banks in California are Japanese-owned.

And On It Goes

Financial services closely related to banking and securities are next on the target lists of the Japanese juggernauts. JCB, the largest Japanese credit card, was launched in 1961 by Sanwa Bank when there were only 100,000 Japanese travelers abroad. It benefited for years by collaboration with American Express. Today, with some 4 million travelers, JCB has abandoned the cooperative agreement with American Express and even plans to compete with them head on. JCB is now represented in 30 countries with over 25,000 outlets, and within two years their infrastructure will spread over 60 countries and some 50,000 outlets.

Leasing is another area where the Japanese are looking for expertise. Sanwa Bank led the assault by luring the Dresdner Bank into a joint venture with the Bank of China for a major leasing company based in Beijing. The Japanese securities houses have already obtained banking licenses in Australia, the U.K. and Luxembourg, begun to operate on the New York Stock Exchange, and penetrated somewhat smaller financial markets such as Amsterdam, Hong Kong and Singapore. They gained entry through shrewd political manoeuvering and bilateral agreements whereby the Japanese were able to offer something in order to get concessions in return. A good example is the trade-off of two seats for British brokers on the Tokyo Stock Exchange, in return for a seat on the London Stock Exchange *and* a commercial banking license in London for Nomura Securities Company. It is interesting to observe Japan's Ministry of Finance working so diligently to promote activities of Japanese financial houses abroad which would be prohibited to those same firms by MoF regulations at home!

It will not be long before we hear charges that "The Japanese are dumping financial services." In fact, the Chairman of Barclays Bank has already leveled an open accusation against them for doing just that. The Japanese are currently offering loans at only $\frac{1}{16}$% over cost, and their fees for funds management are only 0.55% when the market standard is 1%. Pressure is mounting on the governments of North America and Europe to negotiate "voluntary" restraint agreements with the Japanese in financial services, just as was done in semiconductors and in textiles, steel, and autos before that. And just as with those other industries, protectionism in financial services will inevitably allow the Japanese to raise their profit margins and to use the additional capital for extended joint ventures and straightforward acquisitions abroad, thus strengthening and further consolidating their global dominance in financial services.

Outlook

As long as governments, the consumer and the sector concerned know that they have to face up to the Termite Strategy, it is possible to design effective counter-strategies. But unless we understand their strategy, we will design the wrong policies, ask for protection which will not help, and seek cooperative arrangements which will result in the draining of our expertise to our major competitors.

Like termites, the Japanese are building up their financial services "empire", functioning quite independently and efficiently, offering cost-effective quality products and services, with expertise and profits flowing back home. Though there may be no master plan, the *benefits* are nonetheless centrally controlled by Mother Japan. The vulnerable financial houses of the West are slowly but steadily being eaten away by the Japanese; their very foundations will be eroded unless we undertake the survival tactics to counter the thousands of steps applied by those cash-rich, profit-hungry, long-term-oriented financial powerhouses.

CHAPTER 9
Survival Tactics

At first glance, it is easy for us in the West to shrug off or even to welcome the new expansion of the Japanese financial service houses. After all, if they are willing to supply us with large amounts of capital at cut-rate prices, why complain? Who isn't glad to get his money cheaper? But beyond that immediate boon to the consumer of funds, the threat of Japanese dominance of global financial services is real and substantial.

A first consequence is the obvious—though often overlooked—fact that the piper must eventually be paid. As the United States and the other industrialized countries of the West move away from their traditional capital self-sufficiency or even capital export positions toward mounting financial indebtedness to Japan, so do our obligations for future payments of interest, dividends, principal and service fees to the Japanese mount relentlessly. Unless these payment obligations are matched by corresponding increases in real productivity—a most unlikely prospect—then more and more of our productive energy and that of future generations will be devoted to servicing our financial obligations to the Japanese. Moreover, as our western economies become increasingly dependent upon sustained financial support from the Japanese, so we become more vulnerable to economic and political influences from Japan. Is the West an "underdeveloping" part of the globe? It is no exaggeration to say that we Americans and Europeans are slipping toward a position of financial dependence not unlike that suffered today by many so-called Third-World countries.

Still more insidious is the long-term threat to the economic vitality and entrepreneurial spirit of Americans and Europeans. As our domestic financial institutions fall increasingly under direct Japanese control, as they surely will if current trends continue, the highest level, highest value-added financial skills—planning, strategy formulation, engineering complex financial packages, even finance-related technological developments—will be increasingly centred in Tokyo or Osaka. We in the West are being left with the middle- and lower-level skills: less creative, less innovative, less profitable. Do we really want to allow ourselves to slip into such a subservient position vis-a-vis the Japanese?

Table 9-1 identifies specific elements of the Japanese challenge and summarizes, for each, appropriate responses both for private firms and for governments in North America and Europe. The reader will find it useful to refer frequently to the Table while reading the discussion below.

The Survival Tactics

The Japanese CHALLENGE	Private sectors' RESPONSE	Governments' RESPONSE

Awareness and Complacency

The Japanese CHALLENGE	Private sectors' RESPONSE	Governments' RESPONSE
1 The Japanese do not publicize their business strategies, market successes or long term objectives	1 Avoid complacency about present strengths and market position	1 Be aware of the long term implications of Japan's Second Wave on trade and employment at home

Long-term Strategic Positioning

The Japanese CHALLENGE	Private sectors' RESPONSE	Governments' RESPONSE
2 The Japanese target their strategies on the basis of their strengths and the competitors' weaknesses	2 Identify new long term profit centers on the basis of an objective strengths-and-weaknesses analysis and focus on new opportunities emerging in a changing market	2 Develop a comprehensive and finely tuned statistical framework and identify areas of potential comparative advantages
3 The Japanese selectively phase out non-competitive industries and services and focus on high value-added activities	3 Drop traditional business activities with little future or that are prone to price cutting competition	3 Assist in the fragile reconversion to facilitate the phasing out of traditional low value-added activities

101

The Survival Tactics

Strategic Alliances

The Japanese CHALLENGE	Private sectors' RESPONSE	Governments' RESPONSE
4 The Japanese have access to a large home market controlled by highly diversified keiretsu groups	4 Apply a strategy of networking based on 'common economic interest' offering a one-stop-shopping, instead of financially based acquisitions	4 Create a truly integrated policy for all traditional service sectors: finance, insurance, distribution and trade; and relax anti-trust legislation
5 The Japanese build up an international network, covering the globe	5 Design a transnational network with complementary companies through-out the world	5 Complete the creation of a large integrated internal market across boundaries of like-minded countries
6 The Japanese carefully shield their market from foreign competition. Cooperation with foreign firms is aimed at acquiring know-how for Japan	6 Enter into selective partnerships with Japanese companies securing a fair trade-off between market access/profits and transfer of expertise	6 Adapt national policies safeguarding the home market to the global realities of international cooperation among companies
7 The Japanese apply cutthroat pricing strategies	7 Focus on 'relationship services' aimed at client loyalty instead of transactional services susceptible to price competition	7 Monitor pricing strategies and policies, avoiding discrimination against local financial services

The Survival Tactics

The Japanese CHALLENGE	Private sectors' RESPONSE	Governments' RESPONSE

Creating a Competitive Edge

The Japanese CHALLENGE	Private sectors' RESPONSE	Governments' RESPONSE
8 The Japanese workforce continuously rotates jobs within the keiretsu and benefits from lifetime employment	8 Focus on employee loyalty to the company and continuous training programs, developing a multi-disciplinary work force	8 Relax taxation of financial compensation and profit sharing schemes, and offer incentives for training programs
9 The Japanese keiretsus have both broad experience in financial services and access to state-of-the-art information technologies	9 Financial service companies apply information technologies for the automation of high volume, but low value-added services	9 Governments develop the service infrastructure and secure the compatibility of standards in the home market

Political Engineering

The Japanese CHALLENGE	Private sectors' RESPONSE	Governments' RESPONSE
10 Japanese apply political engineering techniques and strategies offering tit-for-tat deals to selected governments	10 Willingness of the private sector to work closely together with the public institutions both on national and regional level	10 Governments avoid competing against each other for Japanese deals and incorporate officials with a vision of political engineering and its long term impact on trade and employment

Awareness and Complacency

Our worst enemy now is *complacency*. It is easy—too easy—for us to shrug off the Japanese financial challenge with the same platitudes we used a decade ago as the Japanese positioned themselves to gain dominance over so many of our manufacturing industries, from watches and cameras to cars and information technology: "It's a passing phenomenon;" "the Japanese can't really innovate;" "Japanese business is so culture-bound that it will quickly flounder outside of its homeland;" "Our own managers are innovative enough to keep ahead of them;" etc. The Japanese do not publicize their strategies and their competitive successes as we in the West are prone to do. They prefer to keep a low profile, and thus their expansive moves go easily unnoticed. But it is time for our business leaders to open their eyes to the challenge of Japan's Second Wave, to acknowledge that there *is* a threat, and to reshape their competitive strategies accordingly. It is imperative, similarly, that government leaders in North America and Europe be fully aware of the long-term implications of the Second Wave in formulating public policy. The growing Japanese presence may bring short-term economic and political benefits, but what effects will it have in the longer run on our trade balances, on the quality of our employment, and on our innovative abilities?

Long-Term Positioning

Once our own financial institutions shed their complacency and accept that they indeed face a crisis situation, their first critical need is to begin defining more clearly where their potential profit centers for the future lie: in other words, where their productive resources can be focused most profitably for the future. One of the great strengths of the Japanese is their ability to target their competitive energies, focussing on specific niches where their potential strengths are greatest or where the competition is weakest. There are many high-value-added financial activities in which western financial institutions still have a clear-cut edge over the Japanese: trust banking, portfolio management, venture capital, mergers and acquisitions, swap arrangements, and engineering complex financial packages, to name a few. Given our limited resources, we have no choice but to focus our energies toward these and other new niches which will certainly arise in the highly fluid environment of international finance. We cannot assume that we can keep on doing what we have been doing, even though we may do it well.

Keeping one step ahead of the Japanese will mean constantly scanning, innovating, targeting new directions. American and European financial houses certainly are creative enough to do this. After all, nearly all of the significant innovations in financial services to date have originated outside of Japan. The real challenge will be to shift quickly into the new, high-value-added activities as they open up, even at the possible cost of abandoning portions of our more traditional markets to the relentless "termites" gnawing at our heels. This will be difficult, as it will require de-emphasizing or abandoning some familiar activities and markets in which both individuals and institutions have strong vested interests. But the only alternative to focused change is to continue serving our traditional markets behind increasingly restrictive protectionist legislation, raising the cost to consumers and ultimately eroding our competitive abilities even further.

There is no question that the main impetus in countering the competitive challenge of Japanese financial services must come from our own financial service houses themselves. But there is a great deal that governments can do to provide guidance and support, short of interfering directly in the affairs of the private sector. First, they can perform a much more important role in helping the private sector to identify areas of potential comparative advantage. Japan's Ministry of International Trade and Industry (MITI) and other government-sponsored think-tanks perform an invaluable service to Japan's private sector by undertaking macroeconomic studies and providing strategic guidance to the private sector. Our western governments can play a comparable role by helping to assemble and support the kinds of high-level research activities needed to identify and define areas of current and future comparative advantage. Government can help the private sector further by developing and disseminating timely, comprehensive, and finely-tuned statistics so that our business managers can formulate their strategies with the best possible information and foresight. Governments also can, in many western countries, play a more supportive role in the delicate process of phasing out traditional low-value-added activities as companies redirect their focus toward the high-growth areas. All of this will require a substantially greater willingness of the public and private sectors to work in tandem than exists currently in some western countries, most notably the United States.

Strategic Alliances

At the same time that our financial institutions face growing competitive pressure to *specialize* their focus into niches of comparative advantage, they face seemingly contradictory market demands for greater *diversification* of the services they offer. It is clear that consumers of

105

services are increasingly demanding "one-stop shopping," i.e., financial service centers capable of providing a broad range of services, from straight financial loans and deposits to equity trading, insurance policies, currency swaps, and travel advice. No individual company is yet equipped to provide such a broad range of services efficiently, regardless of its size. The answer is *alliances:* linkages with other home-based financial institutions offering complementary high-value services. This emphatically need *not* be done through formal mergers or acquisitions. Indeed, the current spate of mergers and acquisitions in our financial service industry—based more on leveraging balance sheets with undervalued assets than on any market strategy guided by complementarity—has sapped the vitality of many companies by tying up huge amounts of capital in nonproductive stock purchases, as well as by demoralizing the organizations involved and causing a flight of personnel. What we need, instead, are *informal* alliances between service firms offering complementary financial services—i.e., banks, insurance companies, brokerage houses, foreign-exchange specialists—all linking up contractually to provide their own specialized services in combination with others. Such alliances will facilitate integration of financial services and fusing of technology, thus improving both efficiency for the companies and service for their customers. The resulting increases in scale, scope and efficiency can provide a substantial counterweight to the Japanese onslaught.

A related type of productive alliance is with other cash-based service companies such as retail stores, aimed at securing access for financial services to new mass-distribution and even electronic-distribution channels. Such alliances help bring organizational economies of scale to the firms involved, increasing their productivity and better serving the convenience of the consumer. Again, we have only to look at the highly-diversified *keiretsu* or economic-interest groups in Japan to see how successfully diversification via collaboration among complementary, like-minded companies can enhance international competitiveness. Such alliances need not, of course, be confined by national boundaries. Transnational cooperative networks could logically begin on a regional basis—for example, alliances spanning the European Community or North America.

A major re-thinking of the traditional policies of many western governments will be required if such alliances are to be effectively realized by the private sector. The first need is for truly integrated national policies spanning all of the service sectors. This will require a more sophisticated political leadership than we have in many western countries today. Politicians are accustomed to viewing the different sectors of financial services at the level of the four pillars: commercial banking, investment banking, trust banking, and insurance. But market forces are rapidly breaking these distinctions down; and within each sector there exist many different sub-sectors, each responsive to very different kinds of stimulation and encouragement. We need leadership able to understand these fine distinctions and the policy implications which may result. Moreover, we need people in charge at the government level who can grasp the whole picture: it is not just finance that is involved, but also very complex interfacings with governmental policies regarding employment, trade, technology, etc. It is precisely the ability of the Japanese government to provide such high-level economic guidance and coordination that constitutes one of the real strengths of the Japanese business system. We cannot afford to ignore it.

We will almost certainly have to relax some of our anti-monopoly legislation if we are to successfully encourage the kinds of cooperative linkages among our own financial houses which may be needed to square off against the enormously concentrated strength of the Japanese. We will also need more progress in creating large, integrated internal markets for financial services across boundaries of like-minded countries. Completion of an open internal market for financial services for the twelve member countries of the European Community by 1992, and the prospect of free trade in financial services between the U.S. and Canada offer a basis for development in which smaller financial houses can be exposed to larger markets than at present without being thrown into the full winds of global competition.

Multinational Collaborative Arrangements

An even more far-reaching type of alliance could be cooperative working relationships among potential competitors of different nationalities, including the Japanese themselves. In other words, if we can't beat them, why not work *with* them, combining our financial skills and marketing expertise with their access to capital and their placement channels to provide the most efficient possible symbiotic combination of comparative advantages? At first glance, the idea of forming alliances with competitors may seem preposterous. But that is exactly what is happening in some of the major manufacturing sectors, most notably automobiles. Who would have thought a few years ago that we would ever see the networks of global working alliances that exist today among General Motors and Toyota for example, or between Chrysler and Mitsubishi or Nissan, Volkswagen, and Alfa Romeo? The important point here is that it is possible to achieve mutually-productive working relationships on an international scale on the basis of cooperative agreements short of formal mergers or acquisitions, thus helping to maintain the independence and integrity of each of the participating institutions.

The most striking example of collaborative potential between Japanese and westerners in financial services was the announcement in March 1987 that American Express would sell a 13% stake in its Shearson Lehman Brothers securities operation for $530 million to Nippon Life Insurance Co. This follows Sumitomo Bank's earlier purchase of a 12.5% investment in Goldman Sachs for $500 million (although the latter deal excluded a direct equity link). The latest move links together some of the most massive players in the financial services industry: American Express is one of the world's largest international financial services conglomerates, with a stock market capitalization of $17 billion ($3\frac{1}{2}$ times larger than Merrill Lynch and more than twice as big as Citicorp, the largest U.S. money-centre bank); Nippon Life is the largest of Japan's huge insurance companies; and Shearson is the third-largest Wall Street investment bank. Shearson Lehman and Nippon Life will cement their new relationship with a joint venture in London which will concentrate on investment advisory work and asset management. It is expected to be the first of several projects involving American Express, Shearson and Nippon Life in "key financial centers of Asia and other regions of the world."(1)

The trick in such cross-national collaborative arrangements with the Japanese is, of course, to ensure that the long-term gains to the two sides are really balanced. Too often in the past, such arrangements appear to have helped the Japanese to gain significant competitive advantages by giving them access to valuable skills, while offering the American and European partners little in return except short-term infusions of capital, or potential market access of dubious value. Reich and Mankin, in their article on collaborative arrangements cited earlier, concluded that:

> The big competitive gains come from learning about...processes—and the result of the new multinational joint ventures is the transfer of learning from the United States to Japan.(2)

There are indications that westerners are beginning to scrutinize much more carefully the trade-offs involved in collaborative arrangements with the Japanese. A major objective of Sumitomo's acquisition of 12.5% of Goldman Sachs—to acquire skills in investment banking—was thwarted, for example, when American officials refused to permit Sumitomo to send trainees to Goldman's New York offices, on the pretext that such activity would violate the statutory separation of commercial and investment banking.

Creating a Competitive Edge

While intercompany alliances may help western firms achieve the scale and scope needed to effectively confront the Japanese, our business managers can do much more to sharpen the competitive edge of their financial service houses. We have emphasized throughout this book the cut-throat competitive pricing strategies used by Japanese financial service companies. Our western firms cannot realistically hope to compete head-on with the Japanese giants in price competition, for two reasons. First, they do not have access to seemingly-inexhaustible supplies of low-cost funds as the Japanese do. Moreover, our western emphasis on short-term profit performance precludes most financial houses from sustaining for any substantial period of time the low earnings which price-cutting usually implies. To compete with the Japanese, our western financial firms will have to focus more on *relationship* services aimed at client loyalty, rather than on transactional services susceptible to price competition. What this boils down to is a more *market*-oriented approach to winning and holding the loyalty of our financial customers, be they individuals or corporations. If our financial institutions provided optimal service within a long-term framework of confidence, most customers would not turn their backs for a mere one-half or one-quarter percent. We seem not to have that kind of relationship now.

More can be done also in the internal management of our financial institutions, particularly in human resource management. One of the main strengths of our Japanese competitors is their low labor turnover and the extremely strong loyalty of their employees. Cultural differences clearly preclude the same degree of company devotion in most western societies. There is, nevertheless, a great deal we can learn in terms of recruiting, training, job security, and employee participation that could help western companies improve their long-term productivity. Our financial institutions may not have the mountains of cash that the Japanese have, but we do have a proven level of creativity and entrepreneurship. Our ability to motivate personnel through new approaches, such as profit-sharing schemes that will give larger numbers of employees a feeling of partnership and shared accomplishment, will be a key determinant of our success in countering the challenge of the Second Wave. Once again, governments can help with creative tax changes designed to encourage profit-sharing schemes, and with substantial incentives for corporate training programs.

Building and maintaining an effective competitive edge will require also a significant change in the attitudes of western shareholders and investors. The relentless demands placed on our financial institutions for short-term profit performance constitute one of their most serious handicaps in facing the Japanese. While our best route to meeting the Japanese challenge is clearly not to try to match their price competition head-on, our financial service companies could nevertheless compete much more effectively if they were more able to develop strategies based on long-term growth and market share considerations, just as the Japanese do, thus enhancing their ability to engage the Japanese on their own terms where appropriate.

By identifying and pursuing new profit opportunities; by forming effective alliances with other service companies both at home and abroad; by attending to the needs of both employees and customers; our financial service firms can do much more to develop client relations that are strong and loyal. We can create our own captive markets, through a market approach, just as the Japanese are doing. But to sustain any real competitive edge, our private sector needs one other vital ingredient that Japan's banks and securities houses can safely rely on: a sympathetic and supportive government policy environment.

This does *not* mean protectionism. It should be clear from our earlier attempts to cope with Japanese manufacturing competition that protectionism is not a viable long-run solution: we've tried it before and it simply hasn't worked. There are far more Japanese cars entering the U.S. and Europe today than there ever were before, despite a variety of protectionist moves; and current attempts by the U.S. government to block the inflow of low priced Japanese semiconductors will almost certainly weaken the long run competitive position of America's high-tech industries. Nor are other traditional avenues of government support such as investment credits or direct cost subsidies likely to contribute much to a lasting competitive edge in financial services, where the productive activity and the nature of costs differ so from those of manufacturing.

But there are areas in which governments *can* play an effective role. First, they can design tax and employment schemes tailored more specifically to the characteristics and needs of the financial services sector. The need for tax incentives to encourage profit sharing and employee training was mentioned earlier. But the issue is broader. Take investment tax credits as an example. For a traditional manufacturing company whose capital equipment has a ten- or twenty-year life cycle and a correspondingly long-term amortization scheme, it is accepted that government may tax away half its profit. But in a sector where it is difficult even to imagine the concept of a product life cycle, that logic does not apply. Today's financial service institutions are required to invest huge sums of internally-generated funds into training employees whose skills are highly mobile, and into communication facilities which may become obsolete in two or three years in a rapidly-changing market. We need to substantially reshape our taxation schemes to fit the nature of service industries in general, and the needs of financial services in particular, if we are to effectively meet the challenge of the Japanese.

Another area where governments can help is in developing the infrastructure for services. Financial services in Japan are highly concentrated in the giant *keiretsu* groups. Financial service firms benefit directly from the strategic planning which the groups provide, and from their direct access to state-of-the-art technology developed by other firms in the "family." In North America and Europe we have, instead, a multitude of small-scale financial houses which lack such planning abilities and, except for a few giants, do not have direct access to state-of-the-art technology. We need coordinated action between private and public sectors, and much greater public support for development of the financial services infrastructure—data highways, value-added networks, etc.—if we are to stand up against the enormously concentrated strength of the Japanese.

Political Engineering

The Japanese are highly skilled at "political engineering": negotiating bilateral deals with other governments which secure major gains for Japanese financial service firms while often yielding relatively little in return. We have given a number of examples throughout this book: the agreement permitting Nomura Securities Co. to obtain both a brokerage license and a commercial banking license in the lucrative U.K. market in return for Tokyo Stock Exchange seats of dubious value for two British houses; the arrangements in which Japan was opened to foreign trust banks under terms which forced them into one-sided joint ventures; the agreement to stop "dumping" Japanese computer chips in the U.S., raising prices in the U.S. market while still allowing the entry of low-priced Japanese chips via other countries; etc.

Western governments negotiate with the Japanese behemoth from a position of weakness, often vying against one another in tit-for-tat deals which open up entire national markets to the Japanese in return for a concession to an individual national firm—thus ensuring incompatibilities and sub-optimization that ultimately handicap our own financial houses. We need much better coordination among the governments of the western countries to counter the concentrated bargaining strength of "Japan Inc."

111

A Final Word

Meeting the challenge of Japan's Second Wave will require bold new approaches by our financial houses and our governments alike, and most importantly, it will require an extraordinary willingness on the part of the private and public sectors to work together. There is no clear-cut formula or set of steps that we in the West can take to counter the Japanese challenge in financial services. But by being *aware* of the "Termite Strategy"—of *what* is happening, *where* the Japanese are likely to go, and *how* they intend to get there—we will be better prepared to shape our competitive strategies accordingly.

1. "Nippon Life to Pay $530m for Shearson Stake," *Financial Times,* March 20, 1986; "American Express Hunts for a Global Advantage," *Financial Times,* March 25, 1987.
2. Robert B. Reich and Eric D. Mankin, "Joint Ventures with Japan Give Away our Future," *Harvard Business Review,* March-April 1986, p. 78.

Nomura Securities Co

EVERYTHING YOU EVER WANTED TO KNOW ABOUT JAPANESE SECURITIES HOUSES BUT WERE AFRAID TO ASK

An equity base of over $4 billion. Net income of well over $1 billion. $150 billion in assets under custody. 3.9 million customer accounts. It's big and it's real and it's heading our way fast, and it knows what it wants and might very well just get it. It goes by the name of Nomura Securities, and what it wants is your money; money to buy, money to sell, and above all money to reshape, reform, repackage and resell for more than it cost to produce. Nomura stands alone as a giant among giants, a colossus whose stated goal is to be everything to everybody everywhere in the financial services business. Not exactly what you'd call normal strategic planning. But Nomura has not gotten where it is through following the norm; normal planning normally yields normal results. Instead of planning, Nomura has followed a vision, a vision that has foreseen what the market would want, what that meant in terms of products that Nomura would have to offer, and how those products would have to be produced and delivered. The rapidly changing technological and financial environment of the last decade has enabled Nomura to steer its way to the front of an industry not known for its kindness to the uncompetitive. The prospect of a further explosion of deregulation in international financial markets will give Nomura the chance to prove its mettle, to see if indeed it can gain and hold onto the top spot in this dynamic service industry.

Nomura had its beginnings in 1925 when Mr. Tokushichi Nomura decided to open up a brokerage house in Osaka, based on the novel idea that sound research could take much of the risk out of what was at that time a highly speculative brokerage industry in Japan. Mr. Nomura was the first in Japan to visit firms, examine their books, interview managers and workers in order to assess the firm's condition before delivering detailed analyses to clients. This habit of being the first to offer superior information services to clients proved to be a most successful guiding principle in Nomura's drive to the top.

Staying at the Forefront

Today, that initial investment in research has blossomed into NRI – Nomura Research Institute – the largest think tank of any kind in Japan, established with the assistance of Stanford Research Institute. Ordinary financial analysis remains a pillar of strength in the NRI edifice, of course. Over 1,300 firms listed on the Japanese stock exchange are continuously monitored and updated. IRAD – Institutional Research and Advisory Department – is a special department with NRI designed to target their research towards some 300 high-growth firms in electronics, biotechnology, robotics, pharmaceuticals and other industries with an eye to presenting these attractive opportunities to foreign investors.

This pioneering research capability has allowed Nomura to be first among its Japanese peers in introducing new products, Nomura was the first Japanese securities firm to underwrite bonds, and continued to promote a wide variety of other debt securities to customers worldwide, including straight bonds, convertible bonds, and foreign CP's and CD's. Nomura also handled CD's and foreign currency-denominated bonds in the domestic market after the lifting of restrictions in 1985. Nomura lead-managed the first public offering by the World Bank, the first Euroyen issue by a private corporation (Sony), and the first Euroyen issue by a private foreign corporation (Dow Chemical). In addition, Nomura began to displace the notion of Japanese financial firms strong in capital and placement power but lacking in creativity through innovative financial deals, the most spectacular of which being the "Heaven and Hell" swap for IBM in 1985.

Responding to a perceived need in the marketplace, Nomura has pioneered investment trust business in Japan. The Nomura Securities Investment Trust Management Company was created in order to offer savings-conscious Japanese consumers the opportunity to invest in securities. In 1980, Nomura introduced the Medium-term Government Bond Fund, Japan's first equivalent of a money market fund. Later, Nomura even offered foreign funds managed concurrently with overseas firms. With innovative approaches, Nomura Securities Investment Trust Management Co. has grown to become Japan's largest investment trust management firm. Total assets under management at the end of 1985 totalled more than ¥4.2 trillion.

Research and product development are key ingredients for success in the financial services industry, but technology has the potential to revolutionize the way in which customers receive and use those services. Recognizing that, Nomura took steps to meet the challenge, resulting in the creation in 1966 of NCS – Nomura Computer Systems – today the largest data processing service company in Japan, staffed by over 1,000 specialists.

In 1982 Nomura came out with CAPITAL – Computer Aided Portfolio and Investment Total Analysis – a highly efficient, on-line global information system first introduced domestically in Japan before being expanded internationally a year later. CAPITAL delivers what NRI produces. Subscribers can instantly call up a broad range of data on all Japanese markets, detailed analyses of firms in all South East Asian financial centres, and macro-economic surveys of the Asia Pacific region, in both graphic colour and tabular form. This is an unparalleled capability for this region of the world, a key marketing tool for approaching foreigners keen on investing in the increasingly important Pacific Basin. Plans for the future include extension of CAPITAL data bases to include information on American and European securities, to ensure that Nomura has a hand in the flow of funds out of Japan as well as in.

An international focus is nothing new to Nomura. A 50/50 balance between international and domestic operations has long been a cherished goal. In 1927, Nomura was the first Japanese securities firm to establish a branch office overseas, in New York. In the 1960's and 1970's, Nomura expanded its international network to 29 offices in 27 cities to maintain a presence in all of the world's major financial centres.

First Japan . . . and then the World

In 1969 NSI – Nomura Securities International – was formed in New York specifically to exploit opportunities present in the American market. From a strictly Japanese securities trading operation NSI has grown into a major force in the American financial community, having gained a seat on the New York Stock Exchange in 1981 and more recently primary dealer status with the U.S. Federal Reserve Board, a difficult and highly prestigious status to achieve. Besides dealing in U.S. securities, NSI is active in leading American clients to Japan's fast-growing equity markets. Recent noteworthy achievements include a first yen-denominated issue for Fannie Mae in the U.S. market and the first Euroyen bond issue by a Japanese firm, Sony.

NIMCO – Nomura Investment Management Company – and its North American subsidiary NCM – Nomura Capital Management – were created in 1981 to provide investment advice and portfolio management services to foreign institutional investors such as central banks and pension funds through its link with NRI. This link gives NCM a very strong research background, particularly for clients interested in the Asia Pacific region. NCM now has offices in New York, Toronto and Sao Paulo, with assets under management having risen from US $700 million to US $6 billion in 1986. NCM has succeeded in snapping up some of the best names as clients, including General Electric, General Motors, Eli Lilly, the Employees Retirement System of the State of Hawaii, the State of Oregon, South Western Bell and the Frank Russel Trust Company.

In Europe, Nomura has taken advantage of a less restricted environment than exists in Japan to engage in a smørgasbord of investment banking activities, including corporate finance, brokerage, underwriting, banking services and other securities businesses. From a representative office opened in London in 1964, Nomura's European presence has spread to Amsterdam, Brussels, Stockholm, Frankfurt, Zurich, Geneva, Lugano and Paris, all under the umbrella of Nomura International based in London. Nomura has succeeded in lead-managing over 35% of the corporate bond issues of Japanese companies in Europe, and is currently aiming at the formation of venture business, fund procurement for expansion of plant and equipment, and mergers and acquisitions advice. With European financial centres boldly venturing forth into uncharted deregulated waters, Nomura is well positioned to expand into other financial services.

In Asia, Nomura has strong footholds in the developing financial centres of the region. Hong Kong hosts Nomura International (Hong Kong), which acts as broker, dealer, underwriter, investment advisor, and most recently as deposit-taker following changes in Hong Kong banking laws, making it a complete offshore banker. SNMB – Singapore Nomura Merchant Banking Limited – was created in 1972, and now participates in the Asian dollar capital market as an Asian Currency Unit licensed merchant bank, as well as securities dealings and traditional banking activities. In 1986 all Australasian operations were collected under NAL – Nomura Australia Limited – to serve Australasia's growing capital markets. In the Middle East, Nomura Investment Banking (Middle East) was created in Bahrain in 1982 to channel oil dollars to the world's capital markets. Other Nomura offices in Bangkok, Seoul, and Jakarta serve growing Asia-Pacific economies.

China deserves special mention. Nomura is markedly optimistic about China's future, having been the first securities company to open an office there, and offices currently in Shanghai and Beijing. In 1982 Nomura lead-managed China's first yen-denominated bond issue since the revolution, and in 1985 lead-managed all three Samurai bond issues by the Bank of China. Nomura China Investment Company was created in 1985 to act as a bridge between Chinese authorities and Japanese industry in developing trade, technical assistance, and investment. As free market policies expand the Chinese economy, Nomura will keep expanding its financial services to meet the increasing needs.

Variety: the Spice of Life

Nomura has diversified into other related financial services almost as fast it has expanded geographically. In 1973 JAFCO – Japan Associated Finance Company – was established to engage in venture capital activities, and is now Japan's largest venture capital business with 40% of the market. JAFCO also has offices in California, Hong Kong, Singapore, and a representative office in London. In 1986 Nomura teamed up with Babcock & Crown Inc., a leader in U.S. tax-based financing, to create Nomura Babcock & Crown. The new firm engages in syndicating and coordinating the completion of major tax-oriented financing, and will probably use Babcock's expertise in leasing and Nomura's contacts in order to do business with China. JAMCO – Japan Associated Mortgage Acceptance Company – was created in 1983 to specialize in financing related to mortgage securities, consulting in real estate financing, and to act as an agent for property insurance companies. Nomura Real Estate Development Company was established in 1957 to plan and sell residential developments, manage a portfolio of commercial and residential investment properties, and provide a full range of real estate-related services. Nomura Card Services Company was established in 1985 to provide credit card and personal loan services. Nomura Tourist Bureau was created in 1973 to provide domestic and overseas travel and tourism services. Nomura Real Estate has worked itself up to number three on the national market.

Conclusion

We can see that Nomura is not content to rest on its laurels; it wants to be everywhere at the same time. It is in the process of creating a new industry group with numerous satellite companies gravitating around the leader, Nomura Securities. As deregulation eases the barriers between banks and securities companies in Japan, new dangers and opportunities will be confronted. Nomura has a history of thriving in such a changing environment.

Nomura's previous president has succinctly summarized Nomura's goals for the future: "We'd like to be like Deutsche Bank domestically, Citibank in our penetration of the international market, and Salomon Brothers in our trading capabilitites." They're well on their way to getting all three.

Sumitomo Bank

SELLING UNDERPRICED SERVICES THROUGH
THE ACQUISITION OF OVERPRICED ASSETS

In 1977 the Osaka-based Sumitomo Bank faced a banker's worst nightmare: one of its largest clients, Ataka & Company, faced bankruptcy. The news quickly sent a wave of shock and fear through the Japanese financial community. The situation was particularly nasty for Sumitomo given the traditional Japanese banking custom of honouring all their clients' financial commitments and swallowing large losses rather than losing face and prestige by letting a major client go under. Although Ataka didn't go under, thanks to a hastily arranged merger with another trading giant, C. Itoh Company, Sumitomo was forced to absorb a staggering ¥200 billion in loan losses in order to make the deal go through. In the process Sumitomo lost its position as the most profitable bank in Japan, plunging to eighth position.

In the aftermath, Sumitomo took drastic measures to ensure that such a catastrophe could not and would not be repeated. An American consultancy firm was called in and given a broad mandate to transform Sumitomo into a sleek, modern, Western-style bank. The dramatic restructuring plan that followed organized the bank into domestic, corporate, and international divisions, with an unprecedented focus on international activities. This focus was designed to alleviate the problems of low loan margins and restricted activities in Japan and increased internationalization of funds procurement by both Japanese and foreign firms.

The programme was remarkably successful. In just four years Sumitomo regained its position as the most profitable bank in Japan, a position it has jealousy guarded ever since. In the year ending March 1986 it had the lowest ratio of operating expenses to operating income, the second highest number of loans and deposits per branch, and the highest deposits and net profit per employee of all the Japanese city banks. It ranks fourth worldwide based on total assets. And complementing its powerful base of 223 domestic branches is an international network spanning some 30 nations consisting of 59 offices. From the ashes of disaster grew the roses of success.

A Competitive Edge at Home

In Japan, one of Sumitomo's ambitions is to become the leader in domestic retail banking. Sumitomo sees retail banking operations as a key element in maintaining and improving the bank's profitability, and has continued to strengthen its activities by expanding its retail network. The merger in 1986 between Sumitomo and Heiwa Sogo Bank gave Sumitomo another 103 domestic branches, making it the second largest bank in Japan in terms of deposits, second only to Dai Ichi Kangyo. The merger strengthened enormously Sumitomo's retail base in the Tokyo metropolitan area and signaled a new era of intensified competition between banks for the business of individuals and small and medium sized firms. This bold move was matched by Sumitomo's constant innovations in new product development. For example, in June 1985 the bank announced a new integrated account which includes savings, term deposit, overdraft, and government bond services, offering convenience and flexibility to the consumer while at the same time increasing his borrowing power. Another first is the "Gold Price Guaranteed Service", introduced in 1986, whereby for a small fee customers can buy and sell gold and insure the market value of gold for up to one year, protecting them in the event of an unwelcome price movement. These and other innovations keep Sumitomo one step ahead of the competition.

In the domestic corporate market, Sumitomo continues to stress the importance of maintaining the traditionally strong ties with its corporate customers, through its RM—Relationship Management—teams. RM teams are designed to provide services tailored to the specific needs of individual firms, through electronic cash management and domestic and international investment planning. Sumitomo has tried to woo the largely ignored small and medium-sized corporate market in Japan through the introduction of services such as a revolving credit line for small companies that provide them with greater flexibility in their financial planning. This is a totally new concept in Japan.

In the domestic securities market, Sumitomo has been one of the most active underwriters of government-guaranteed bonds, with a volume of ¥494.3 billion (US $2.75 billion) in 1985, up 10.5% from the previous year. Sumitomo has also become a major player in the secondary market for public bonds following the opening of this market to commercial banks in 1984. Trading volume in this market reached ¥50,083.9 billion (US $278.9 billion) during the fiscal year 1985, with profits of ¥12,700 million (US $70.7 million). To further strengthen its securities business, Sumitomo has acquired 5% of Meiko Securities, a full-service securities underwriter and stockbroker. Although Sumitomo is limited by law to holding only 5% of a stockbroker, it effectively wields control of Meiko through the holdings of industrial companies that have relationships with the bank. Sumitomo expects to expand its domestic securities business further as quickly as the speed of deregulation in Japan permits.

The International Pacesetter

Sumitomo has not forgotten its interest in retail banking activities in its quest for internationalization. Like the other Japanese banks, it has chosen California as home base for retail banking operations in the U.S. With the seventh largest economy in the world, a substantial Japanese-American community, a large Japanese manufacturing presence, and Japan as its leading trade partner, California is an obvious choice for Japanese banks setting up operations overseas. Sumitomo has set up the Sumitomo Bank of California to develop consumer finance, commercial banking, retirement planning and trust banking activities. The Bank's head office in San Francisco surveys the activities of some 50 branches, and with total assets of close to $3 billion, the bank stands as the eighth largest bank in the state. After an initial price-cutting strategy to gain business yielded disappointingly low profits ($7.6 million) in 1982, Sumitomo Bank of California shifted its focus towards better asset and liability management and better asset quality rather than quantity in lending. Profits have risen to $12.9 million in 1985.

International corporate banking activities are served by Sumitomo's strong international network, which Sumitomo has astutely developed with an eye to the future. As an example, Sumitomo now has no less than four representative offices in China to serve that market as it grows. In 1985 Sumitomo continued its ascension in the international loans market with several impressive accomplishments: Sumitomo was the only Japanese bank chosen by London-based Hanson Trust to participate in the £1 billion sterling acquisition of the Imperial Group, and Sumitomo Bank New York branch led a group of 14 Japanese banks in providing a US $250 million credit support for the real estate developer Olympia & York for the US $750 million financing of the World Financial Center Towers B & D, one of the first and largest commercial paper programmes for construction financing.

Sumitomo Bank participates in international lease financing through Sumitomo Bank General Leasing Company, Ltd (SBGL), a domestic affiliate and six overseas leasing affiliates, SB General Leasing (Hong Kong) Co. Ltd; SB General Leasing (Singapore) Pte Ltd; SB General Leasing (U.S.A.) Inc.; SB General Leasing (U.K.) Ltd, Bumiputra Lloyds

Leasing Berhad in Malaysia, and P.T.B.E.I. General Leasing Company in Indonesia. These affiliates provide both domestic and international customers with a range of leasing services. During the fiscal year 1984, Sumitomo Bank was involved in a ￥10 billion international lease for Telefonica (Spanish Telephone Corporation). SBGL was the lead manager.

Project financing is somewhat of a Sumitomo specialty. The Bank has been involved for many years in helping international clients prepare appropriate financing plans with the help of a sophisticated computer model developed in-house specifically to minimize risk while maximizing return on investment. Noteworthy deals include a US $420 million loan to Canada Pechiney Quebec Aluminium Development and a US $300 million loan to UNIMAR Financing Corporation in 1984, and management of a US $650 million loan to Noralco Limited (Elf Aquitaine) and a US $1.65 billion loan to Woodside Oil Limited in 1985.

Merchant Banking: "If you cannot beat them, buy them"

Although Sumitomo has continued to develop the more traditional retail and commercial banking activities, it is in merchant banking that Sumitomo has stood out as a player worth watching. Sumitomo is best known for two deals for its own account that took the world financial community by surprise: the purchase of a controlling interest in the Swiss Banco del Gottardo in 1984, and the even more stunning agreement with Goldman Sachs in 1986 to sell 12.5% of its equity to Sumitomo for a staggering $500 million. In both deals Sumitomo is counting on vaulting itself into the ranks of the top investment banks worldwide by capitalizing on the assets and abilities of their new partners.

In Europe, the Banca del Gottardo deal provides Sumitomo with an ideal means of following their tradtional Japanese clients who are migrating to the Swiss capital markets. There, they can take advantage of lower fees and interest rates for funds procurement than exist in Japan. Gottardo engages in commercial, investment, and private banking, including asset management, precious metals trading, securities underwriting, equipment leasing, and forfaiting. In the domestic bond market, Gottardo is a member of the permanent syndicates and is well-known for its strong placement power thanks to a large asset management business. This asset management expertise and experience is extremely useful to Sumitomo in breaking into Japanese trust management in a roundabout manner, since they are prohibited from entering the market directly. In 1985, Banca del Gottardo maintained a strong presence in the

121

international bond market, participating in 732 public issues worth a total of SwF1.61 billion, up from SwF1.33 billion in 1984. The linkage with Gottardo will help Sumitomo expand into Euro-commercial paper underwriting in the future.

Gottardo complements an existing network of Sumitomo subsidiaries involved in the international securities business: Sumitomo International Finance A.G. (SIF), based in Switzerland; SIF's London branch, Sumitomo Finance International (SFI); Sumitomo Finance (Middle East) E.C. (SFME); Sumitomo International Finance Australia Limited (SIFA); and Sumitomo Finance (Asia) Limited (SFA). These subsidiaries allow Sumitomo to circumvent the Japanese Ministry of Finance "Three Bureau Guidance" rules: under this guidance, when a Japanese bank's overseas subsidiary manages an international public bond issue for a Japanese corporation, a Japanese securities firm has to be brought into the transaction in a leading position. New floating rate instruments such as floating rate notes (FRN's), note issuance facilities (NIF), and revolving underwriting facilities (RUF) have allowed Sumitomo to grow at a tremendous pace. In 1985, Sumitomo was ranked the world's leading manager in NIF's, having managed 208 international bond issues worth US $33.5 billion, an 80% increase from the previous year. Highlights included a US $450 million NIF issue for Houston Natural Gas Corporation, and a US $500 million floating rate note issue by Banque Extérieure d'Algérie, for both of which SFI acted as lead manager. In the Euroyen market, decreased regulation has permitted SFI to take a more active role, resulting in lead and co-management of 25 issues worth ¥475 billion in 1985.

The Goldman-Sachs deal was the first major linkage between a Japanese Bank and a top-rung investment bank. Opinion is divided within the financial community as to whether Sumitomo might have given itself a raw deal. Sumitomo effectively put up $500 million, over half of Goldman Sachs capital, to get only 12.5% of the profits. In addition, Goldman Sachs has made it clear that the direction of the company will not change with the arrival of Sumitomo. However, it should be pointed out that like most Japanese financial institutions, Sumitomo follows a long-term view, and accordingly looks for opportunities that fit in with their long-term strategy. Through this link-up with Goldman Sachs, Sumitomo will have access to important information and sophisticated financial techniques that will prove useful in the domestic Japanese market as it opens up to deregulation. Besides the participation in Goldman-Sachs business and profits, the two firms will form a subsidiary in London to engage in securities activities, and will provide Sumitomo with access to new activities such as corporate finance, mergers and acquisitions, and bond and currency trading. Sumitomo is also using Goldman Sachs to break into the tightly regulated Japanese securities market, where Goldman Sachs has just received a highly coveted seat on the Tokyo Stock Exchange.

Sumitomo has recognized the importance and potential of interest rate and currency swaps, and has accordingly increased the number of swap specialists in key offices worldwide to develop this business. Despite intense competition, Sumitomo's currency and interest rate swap activities amounted to US $1.73 billion in 1984, a fourfold increase from the previous year. And during 1985, it managed to increase its swap activities another 50% over 1984's level.

Summary

Sumitomo's international focus and its bold moves in forming partnerships and alliances with other major market players such as Banca del Gottardo and Goldman Sachs depict an unusually bold and aggressive financial institution. These moves have paid off handsomely for Sumitomo, providing consistently superior performance over its Japanese rivals. Sumitomo appears ready and willing to assume the role of a global financial institution, and is constantly upgrading its capabilities to respond fully to the securitization trend in worldwide financial markets, while at the same time not ignoring the possibilities inherent in introducing new banking technology and innovative financial instruments to a supposedly "saturated" retail banking business. The next major development will be the further opening of the Tokyo financial market to increased competition, both from within and outside. By accurately gauging these trends and by laying down the required infrastructure in offices, people and technology in advance, Sumitomo should stand a good chance of maintaining its reputation as "the best Japanese bank".

APPENDIX 3
Developments in Financial and Capital Markets in Japan (as of August 6, 1986)

Present Share	Planned Steps	Implications	Problems unsolved
(1) EUROYEN BONDS & EUROYEN LOANS *(Euroyen Bonds)* —In addition to international organizations and foreign governments, A– or higher-rated foreign enterprises have been authorized to issue Euroyen bonds since April 1, 1986; foreign banks, if A– or higher-rated, have also been authorized to do so since June 1, 1986.		About 60 foreign manufacturers are newly eligible for issuing Euroyen bonds, with total number of such firms increasing to 220 or so. For foreign banks, especially those operating in Japan, this should lead to a broader base for fund-raising sources.	
—Since April 1, 1986, Japanese businesses have been authorized to issue currency–conversion Euroyen bonds and floating rate Euroyen bonds in addition to fixed rate Euroyen bonds; foreign issuers were permitted to do so in June, 1985.		Japanese corporations could take advantage of foreign exchange and money market conditions, thus promoting their issue of Euroyen bonds.	
—Three Japanese organizations have been recognised as official rating agencies since April 1, 1986 in addition to Standard & Poors and Moodies, U.S.A.		Rating of Japanese corporations should be made easier, thus promoting their issue of Euroyen bonds.	

Present Share	Planned Steps	Implications	Problems unsolved
—The seasoning period of Euroyen bonds has been shortened from 180 days to 90 days since April 1, 1986 except for dual currency bonds.		This is expected to promote trading of Euroyen bonds among Japanese investors thus making it easier for them to purchase such bonds.	
—Withholding tax of 20% imposed on Euroyen bonds issued by Japanese corporations was abolished on April 1, 1985; No withholding tax was imposed on such bonds issued by international organisations and foreign governments and enterprises.		Removal of the tax should lead many of the Japanese companies now eligible to float Euroyen loans to take advantage of that market.	
—Foreign securities companies were authorized to become co-managing underwriters of Euroyen bonds from December 1, 1984; only Japanese securities companies had been authorized to do so until then.		This will help liberalize the underwriting fee for industrial bonds issued in the Japanese market.	
(Euroyen Syndicate Loans) —Euroyen loans extended to non-residents have been completely liberalized since April 1, 1985; Euroyen loans of less than 1 year were liberalized in June, 1984.		This will promote greater offshore trade in yen with less MoF guidance.	Abolition of the ban on mid- and long-term Euroyen Loans to residents.

Present Share	Planned Steps	Implications	Problems unsolved
(2) MONEY MARKET *(Call Market)* —The Bank of Japan has authorized unsecured transactions of two and three weeks' call loans since September 1985; for unconditional and one week call loans, since July 1985.	Unsecured transactions of call loans with longer terms are expected to be authorized in the not-so-far distant future.	This should promote arbitrage transactions with other markets, say, the European market.	
(Certificates of Deposits and Money Market Certifcates) —The minimum issue amount of CDs by Japanese banks and foreign banks operating in Japan was reduced to 100 million yen in April 1985.	The minimum issue amount is expected to be reduced to 50 million yen in the fall of 1986.	Along with other market opening measures, this should contribute to deregulation of interest rates on large deposits.	Further reduction of the minimum issue amount of CDs.
—Maximum amount of CD and MMC issues, in the case of Japanese banks, has been increased to 200% of each bank's equity capital since April 1986, respectively.	The ceiling on those issues is to be increased to 250% from September 1, 1986.	—	
—Foreign banks have been able to issue CDs (in Japan) equivalent to 40% of the combined total of yen-based securities holdings or equivalent to 8 billion yen, whichever is greater, from April 1, 1984	There is expected to be an increase in the ceiling on CD issues by foreign banks.	—	

Present Share	Planned Steps	Implications	Problems unsolved
—The maximum maturity of CDs and the MMCs has been extended from 6 months to 1 year since April 1, 1986, respectively. (The minimum maturity remains one month) —Securities companies have been authorised to deal in CDs since June 1985.	The maximum maturity is to be extended to 2 years by the spring of 1987.	This could lead to the issue of debentures by city banks and the like in the future, who are not permitted to do so.	Issues of CDs and MMCs of less than 1 month.
—Minimum denomination of MMCs stands at 50 million yen now.	Minimum denomination of MMCs is to be reduced to 30 million yen in September 1, 1986.	This step is likely to lead to gradual deregulation of interest rates, including short-term ones.	Further reduction of the denomination of MMCs; removal of or raise the interest rate ceiling on MMCs.
(Treasury Bills) —Treasury bills are at present issued at artificially lower rates than the official discount rate (i.e. Bank of Japan rate).	Establishment of a treasury bill market is under study.	BOJ could manage monetary policy in a more flexible manner and this will have some effect on interest rates over the long-term.	Treasury bill issuance through public auction.
(Bankers Acceptance Market)—A yen based BA market was created on June 1, 1985; securities companies have been permitted to deal since April 1, 1986.		It is hoped that a yen BA market will encourage yen-based exports and imports; the market should be used as a place for short-term fund adjustments. (Use of this market has been very limited so far.)	Trading of dollar-(and other currencies-) based bills in the market; progressive tax rates on yen-based bills drawn by Japanese importers.

Present Share	Planned Steps	Implications	Problems unsolved
(Bond Future Market) —A bond future market was created on October 1, 1985.		It should broaden the scope of transactions on the short-term money market and help improve it.	
(3) CAPITAL MARKET *(Samurai Bonds)* —Since April 1, 1986, A-rated foreign issuers (including international organizations and foreign governments) have been authorized to issue Samurai bonds without limits on amount. (As in the case of Euroyen bonds, there are now 5 rating organizations available for such issuers.)		This gives access to the market for more foreign corporations.	
(Sales and Dealing of Government Bonds) —An additional 46 financial organizations (10 regional banks, 29 mutual banks, 5 credit associations, National Federation of Credit Associations and the Central Bank of Commercial and Industrial Cooperatives) have been authorized to deal in floating government bonds in June 1986, with the result that banks and other financial organizations so recognized total 134 including 9 foreign banks.		Over the longer-term opening the dealing and trading in government bonds should result in these bonds being issued at rates similar to those of private sector and foreign issues.	Underwriting business by foreign banks in the Tokyo market; Deregulation of commission fee for buying and selling in bonds.

Present Share	Planned Steps	Implications	Problems unsolved
(Short-term Government Bonds) —Government bonds with 6 months to maturity have been issued since February 1986.		This could promote arbitrage between long- and short-term interest rate transactions.	
(Membership of the TSE) —10 additional securities companies including 6 foreign ones were approved as members of the Tokyo Stock Exchange on December 24, 1986 (actual membership was granted on February 1, 1986), with member firms now totalling 93.		This could help the TSE to become more international.	Further opening of membership to foreign and Japanese non-member firms; reduction of cost to obtain membership.
(4) INTEREST RATES *(Interest on Large Deposits)* —Interest rates on time deposits of 500 million yen or more have been deregulated on April 1, 1986; interest rates on other deposits are still regulated, controlling the level of interest rates among financial institutions.	Interest rates on time deposits of 300 million yen or more but less than 500 million yen are to be deregulated from September 1, 1986; of 100 million yen or more but less than 300 million yen, from the spring of 1987.	This is expected to promote deregulation of interest rates on smaller deposits.	Postal Savings system, largest deposit regime in world, is independent of MoF/BoJ financial regulation, and controls its own interest rates.

Present Share	Planned Steps	Implications	Problems unsolved
(Interest on Small Deposits) —Interest rates on small deposits are regulated across the board, making no difference among financial institutions.	With the introduction of small MMCs in the next spring, interest rates on small deposits are to be deregulated gradually for the following 3 to 5 years; the deregulation for time deposits will precede that for demand deposits.	Competition for collecting money should be much more severe among financial organizations, including securities companies.	
(5) OTHERS *(Trust Banking)* —9 foreign trust banks have been licensed to participate in the trust banking business in Japan since the fall of 1985.		This should cause increased competition in the pension funds market.	
(Foreign Currencies) —From June 1, 1984, both Japanese banks and foreign banks operating in Japan have been authorized to bring foreign currencies into Japan without limits.		This will lead to a broader base of banking business for foreign banks; Japanese businesses should be able to gain access to cheaper funds.	

130

Present Share	Planned Steps	Implications	Problems unsolved
(Future Trade of Foreign Exchange) —Since April 1, 1984 Japanese (non-financial) corporations have been able to do future trading of foreign exchange regardless of whether: 1) they have concluded contracts on external trade (real demand rule); 2) they have foreign currency-based securities.		This breaks a corporation's dependance on banks for foreign exchange hedging.	
(Tokyo Offshore Market) —there exists no such market in Japan.	A Tokyo offshore market (international banking facility) is to be created in October 1986.	It should promote the internationalization of the yen.	Elimination of "witholding tax" on interest earned and local taxes, to make the offshore market competitive internationally.

Source: Canadian Embassy, Tokyo

Index